# Beowulf:  A Student's Edition

BL Cotton Ms. Vitellius A. XV folio 132 of the Beowulf manuscript, c. 1020
Photo by permission of the British Library

Beowulf

A Student's Edition


translated and introduced
by
E. L. Risden
St. Norbert College


The Whitston Publishing Company
Troy, New York
1994

ISBN 0-87875-455-5

Printed in the United States of America

Contents

# Introduction

One of the great poems in English or any language, *Beowulf* has a simple storyline, but it exhibits many curious facets and interlaces of cultures and concerns, making it an ideal subject for students interested in a variety of fields, from literature to linguistics to history to religion to anthropology. Once thought a mere "thumping good tale of our pagan forebears," *Beowulf* now rates with *Hamlet* and *Moby Dick* among the most often written upon masterpieces of our literary heritage, and it persistently finds its way into college courses from freshman introductions to graduate seminars. Like the work of Shakespeare, Melville, Joyce, and Milton, it continually repays rereading and close attention by yielding up a multitude of linguistic and poetic treasures.

As the first great European poem after the fall of Rome, *Beowulf* would have historical and anthropological significance even if it didn't have literary merit. But in my experience students seldom encounter the poem, in undergraduate or even high school courses, without its leaving at least a ghost or two in their memory. *Beowulf* has a compelling, archetypal power, perhaps because of its antiquity, perhaps because of its style, or perhaps because in dealing with such traditional motifs as life and death, good and evil, the natural and the supernatural, courage and cowardice, and the nature of kingship and heroism--in an exciting tale of swords and sorcery--it delves deeply into our psychological selves and our cultural roots.

The story is recountable in a few lines. Hrothgar, king of the Danes, finds his kingdom troubled by the murderous rampages of the night-beast Grendel. Across the water the Geatish hero Beowulf hears of Hrothgar's plight and comes to his aid. Beowulf awaits the monster in the darkness and grapples with him. Feeling Beowulf's strength, the monster tries to flee, and Beowulf tears Grendel's arm from its socket, after which the creature returns to his lair, a tarn among the mist-slopes, to die. The Danes rejoice, but only briefly, as Grendel's mother appears, taking blood-vengeance by killing one of Hrothgar's favorite counselors. When Beowulf is informed of the murder, he again seeks revenge in single combat, and he enters the haunted mere to battle the she-monster. With the help of a magical sword, he succeeds, freeing the Danes of their misery, and he returns home triumphant to his lord Hygelac. After Beowulf recounts his adventures in Denmark, the story then telescopes fifty years to the time when Beowulf has become king of the Geats and a fire-dragon is awakened by the theft of a cup from his hoard. The dragon attacks a Geatish settlement, leaving it a smoking rubble, but Beowulf again undertakes the quest for vengeance. With the help of his kinsman Wiglaf, Beowulf kills the dragon and wins the hoard, but he is mortally wounded, and he dies leaving his people as likely prey to foreign invaders.

Amidst the central tale the poet has implanted several other short tales or "lays," sometimes referred to as digressions, that show more of the Northern culture from which the story comes: funeral customs, important battles, familial relationships, the position of women in Germanic society. These lays not only contribute to the tone of the poem and give it a sense of epic breadth and historicity, but also reflect on the themes of the poem and the nature of the world of the poem: a violent, transient world where one's hope for immortality lies in heroic courage in action and steadfast loyalty to one's lord, resulting in *lof* and *dom*: fame and glory. At only 3182 lines *Beowulf* is relatively short as epic poems go, but its themes, concerns, and focus on the heroic world and courageous action give it the typical subject matter of primary epics worldwide. Its tone compares more comfortably with Homer and the *Bhagavad-Gita* than with the homilies and biblical poems that dominated its age.

At this point the reader may ask, "Why another translation of *Beowulf?* Don't we already have a dozen good ones?" Several excellent translations remain in print, many useful for students at one level or another. The more accurate are the prose translations (Bradley, Donaldson); the verse translations, often fine poetry (see especially Morgan, Greenfield, Hudson, Rebsamen), tend to sacrifice literal meaning for aesthetic value. Perhaps the best version yet published for student use is Chickering's side-by-side: a fairly accurate translation and copious apparatus accompany the Old English text. Yet the abundance of Chickering's edition may be daunting to the undergraduate or casual reader. In this translation I have sought to fill what I have found to be a gap in the what poets and scholars have done so far: I have aimed at providing the most accurate translation possible, while maintaining readability and keeping in mind the poet's technique and the concerns of interested readers approaching *Beowulf* for the first time.  Everyone has heard the curmudgeonly warning that translations are like spouses:  we cannot expect one that is both beautiful and faithful.  I have courted the faithful one, and I hope have produced one (to borrow the characteristic Anglo-Saxon litotes) that is not entirely unbeautiful.  I have also tried to update the introductory material to include more recent scholarly opinion about the poem's history and meaning.  I hope the student will find herein a text that he or she can trust and enjoy and that will evoke some sense of the poet's time, accomplishments, and imagination.  *Beowulf* is a great and complex poem that deserves the attention of the student and the general reader as well as that of the philologist, and it bears up well under the weight of many interpretations.

## ABOUT THE TRANSLATION

The fact that we have so many renditions of *Beowulf* attests to the difficulty of the task at hand.  One need go no further than the first word of the poem, *Hwaet*, for the beginning of difficulties.  The ancestor of our modern *what*, *hwaet* seems to be a more or less energetic attention-getter, a way of telling an audience that a resitation is about to begin--though it may be no more than a simple *indeed* or *truly*, the way our grandparents often used to preface some announcement with, "Why, did you know that..."

In this particular case (as in some others) I must admit that I have found no accurate way to render the word, since it is purely idiomatic.  I landed on *Hear* because it catches some of the original sound (I could have chosen *Listen*) and because it doesn't sound so foreign to modern ears as *What*? would, though uncompromising accuracy might render something like, "What have I got to say?  This: ...."  Perhaps the closest modern usage that I've noticed is one common among British speakers:  where Americans will often say "Okay" to get an audience's attention and to announce "I'm about to begin," the British speaker will say "Right!"  The sound of that is oddly appropriate, but it would have too much of a Monty Pythonish ring in the context of *Beowulf*.

Of course, *hwaet* does not present the only problem.  Postmodern theorists remind us of the dangers always inherent in translation and interpretation.  As translators or as readers we bring biases and experiences to a text that inevitably color our readings of it.  As a translator of this text I recognize the perils of claiming accuracy, since turning words from one language to another and from one text to another (especially a text separated from us by a thousand years) requires interpretation with every move. Fortunately, modern English has a number of cognates remaining from the Old English of *Beowulf*, so some lines render themselves fairly easily, but even with cognates one must be aware of the possibility of "false friends," words that have undergone semantic drift since the composition of the text, for example a word such as *ceosan* or *geceosan*, the source of our modern verb *choose*, which in Old English may mean *to choose* or occasionally *to accept*, a difference that may affect interpretation or translation. In such instances, I have, of course, had to make an interpretive choice. And then there are those words and phrases debated (even hotly) by scholars, such as *garsecg*, which I take to be a metaphor for the sea, or *ealu-scerwen*, which I believe to be a graphic, physical metaphor for the degree of fear the warriors experience upon Grendel's bursting into Heorot. To deal with such difficult instances, I have, wherever I could, left the term or metaphor in a form close to that which the poet wrote: *garsecg* becomes *wind's-edge* (some scholar's prefer *gar-secg*, *spear-man*, since *gar* literally means *spear*) and *ealu-scerwen* becomes *ale-showers* (some read it as *ale-sharing*). To me, *wind's-edge* and *ale-showers* provide images that show what the poet wanted to achieve and also appear cleary before the modern eye. That way I limit (though I can't eliminate) the amount of interpretation that I force on the text and maximize the opportunity for the student to interpret for himself or herself.

The characteristic Old English verse line consists of two alliterating half-lines, the first usually having two stressed, alliterating syllables, and the second having one or two. I have kept that form whenever I could. Not every line in my translation alliterates as does the original, but the reader will find that the next line will sometimes pick up the sounds of the last, so that the general sound and feel of alliterative verse remains. Where I have caught onomatopoeia or internal rhyme in a line, I have tried to maintain it. I don't believe that the Anglo-Saxon poet thought about meter as such, so I haven't worried about syllable counts; instead, I have tried to keep the number of stresses relatively consistent: the normal, fairly free Old English verse line (composed of two half-lines separated by a caesura, which, since most modern editors inicate by spacing between half-lines, so have I) three or four strong stresses per line, with stressed syllables alliterating. The poet does occasionally use half-lines that to our ears seem to have extra stresses or only one stress, and alliterative patterns vary also. I do believe the poet took care with rhythms, the general ebb and flow, slowing and speeding of the verse, so I have done so as well. Because the manuscript does not capitalize words that refer to God (or gods), I haven't either. Though certain passages may very well refer to the Christian god, I don't feel comfortable asserting that they definately do not suggest Othin or perhaps both Christian and Germanic gods at once, so I have left the lower case, again, so that the reader may choose. I would add finally that apparently for the Anglo-Saxon poet all words that begin with vowels alliterated.

Also, Old English syntax does not always mirror that of modern English; for instance, the Anglo-Saxon poet, possibly because the poem may have originally been composed orally and recited for audiences, uses many appositives, slightly varied restatements of persons or things just named our mentioned. Such statements would allow a poet reciting to get his or her bearings before proceeding with the narrative or simply to give more information or refine or refigure the imagery. The practice often results in a construction that moderns term a dangling modifier, one that will occasionally cause confusion for readers without experience in Old English. I have decided in some instances to smooth the syntax to aid readability; thus, the inquisitive student will not always find that my verses match up half-line by half-line with the original. Sometimes, though, I have kept those appositives/reprises in their original position in the sentence so that the translation will have some of the flavor of the original syntax. The student should realize that the poem is coming from a time distant from our own and in some ways a world different from our own: one that believed in the incantatory power of poetry as well as in dragons.

Finally, the student should know that the manuscript of the poem--only one remains extant--is itself imperfect and sometimes entirely unreadable, having suffered the ravages of time, fire, and scribal inconsistencies and even errors. Every reader of *Beowulf* owes undying gratitude to the generations of scholars who have pored over, edited, and preserved the text so that others could translate, interpret, and enjoy it. Different editors have come to different conclusions about what the text actually *says*; that is, not every word is even clearly transcribable. I have used as my base text the Wrenn-Bolton edition because it is the most recently re-edited. Many scholars prefer Klaeber's edition, and I have in several instances consulted it also. For the student interested in seeing what the manuscript itself looks like, Zupitza's facsimile edition is the readiest source. And to those readers who have a distaste for archaisms: I have introduced none of my own, but have used some of the poet's. Such words as *thane* and *moot* that remain along the fringes of our language will sound familiar to readers of medievalism; I have not added the Elizabethanisms or Victorianisms that often show up in a translator's efforts to give a poem a feel of antiquity, since they would not be true to *Beowulf*, and to be true has been my chief goal. The translation should sound as though the poem has come from the past rather than from Main Street, but it shouldn't sound as though the translator is struggling to make it so.

## ABOUT THE MANUSCRIPT

The single copy of *Beowulf* is part of a manuscript known as Cotton Vitellius A xv. because of its place of storage years ago in Robert Cotton's library--fifteenth book, shelf A, under a bust of the Roman emperor Vitellius. Now on display in the British Museum, it was originally copied onto vellum by two scribes (the second beginning in line 1939) around the year 1020. We don't know who composed the poem originally. Probably in the seventeenth century it was bound in a book, or codex, along with four other Old English pieces: the poem *Judith* and three prose works: *The Passion of St. Christopher*, *The Wonders of the East*, and *Alexander's Letter to Aristotle*. The codex is about 7 1/2 inches long by 4 1/2 inches wide and is now bound in leather. The poem in manuscript bears no title, the title having been suggested later by scholars. Only a large *h* (in the word *hwaet*) decorated with a leaf or sickle shape, followed by a row of slightly enlaged capitals through most of the first half-line, indicates that the poem is beginning. It covers pages (called *folios*) 179-198 in the book according to the earlier numbering, or 132-201 according to the British Museum renumbering. It is divided into 43 sections, called *fitts*, by Roman numerals. In addition to fire damage (in the Cottonian library in 1731) and the crumbling of the edges of some of the pages from age (the edges are now protected with a paper covering), several pages have lacunae or illegible words or passages. In the late eighteenth century the Icelander Grimur Thorkelin and a colleague made two copies of *Beowulf* which have subsequently been useful in determining letters that have since been lost to decay. Two folios, 179 and 198 (following the old numbering), have presented particular difficulty to scholars trying to reconstruct large, murky sections. Some scholars even believe that folio 179 was being at least partially erased and rewritten.

The date and place of origin of the poem have been a consistent source of debate for scholars, but no one has yet solved the problem to the majority's satisfaction. For years the loudest voices stuck to a date around the early eighth century, probably in Mercia or East Anglia; a currently popular opinion (to which I ascribe) runs more to the tenth century, possibly somewhere in the Danelaw. Some hold out for an earlier date (with scant evidence), though others have argued, following careful study of the manuscript, that the manuscript date may also be the date of composition, at least of the poem as we know it.

## MORE ABOUT THE POEM

*Beowulf* probably arose from a long tradition of oral poetry, and it exhibits many of the traits of poems composed orally. For instance, a formal speech almost always begins with a formulaic indicator, such as "Beowulf spoke, son of Ecgtheow," or "Wiglaf spoke, Weohstan's son," and repeated lines or grammatical patterns appear throughout the poem. Epithets also recur in formulaic patterns: "weather-Geats," "war-Geats," "spear-Danes," "east-Danes," "west Danes." Sometimes the variation in the epithet produces alliteration, and sometimes it seems to serve as a pause, as though a poet in the act of orally delivering a poem needed a moment to collect his or her thoughts before going on with the narrative. Seldom do the formulas add new information, though they may occasionally come to a conclusion or pass an almost gnomic judgment: "That was a good king."

A couple of historical anecdotes suggest that if oral poetry was not a regular activity of Anglo-Saxon culture, it was at least not unusual. Bede tells a story of the churchman Aldhelm who sang heroic lays outside his church to draw hearers to mass, and another of the illiterate poet Caedmon, who, after a dream-vision of an angel, composed a brief but beautiful Creation hymn (extant) and, supposedly, a whole batch of biblical poems (unfortunately, lost). And in 797 Alcuin wrote a letter to the Bishop at Lindisfarne to requiring that he stop the singing of pagan poetry during meals: "What has Ingeld to do with Christ?" he asked. In *Beowulf* itself we learn of the "sweet song of the scop," who sings of Creation and also of significant episodes in the histories of important people and peoples. Two scholars, Albert Bates Lord and Milman Parry, traced oral-formulaic composition even into the twentieth century, finding the tradition still active in Yugoslavia. But one must be careful in thinking of *Beowulf* in these terms; though it may have had an oral history, *Beowulf* as we now know it is written, and we study it as a written poem (or at least as a written version), and the act of reading--and reading silently, rather than listening--changes one's experience of it. Despite such limitations *Beowulf* bears up well under reading aloud, and the student who goes to the trouble of learning Old English pronunciation and reciting some of it will be repaid by the opening of another aesthetic dimension that the lover of poetry shouldn't miss.

Another concern of scholars has addressed whether we may consider *Beowulf* a unified whole, a poem, or whether it comprises a collection of lays. In addition to the central narrative of Beowulf's three monster fights, we also find four imbedded historical episodes: the "lay of Sigemund" (lines 874-97), the "Lay of Finn" (1068-1159), the allusion to Modthrytho (1931-62), Beowulf's prophecy of the Danish-Heathobard feud (2020-69). We also find several other seemingly digressive passages. One may suggest that the poem begins with a digression: of Scyld's heroic life and funeral. We also find the Danish scop's Creation song, "Hrothgar's sermon," the whole recapitulation of Beowulf's adventures in Denmark, and the "Lay of the Last Survivor." Each contributes to the poem as a whole. The Sigemund episode provides a comparison with Beowulf and a foreshadowing: the monster-slaying hero who met a tragic end. The Finn episode exemplifies the evils of feuding and blood-revenge. Modthrytho provides an example of a bad queen (as opposed to the good examples of Wealhtheow and Hygd--and the reformed Modthrytho).

Beowulf's prophecy suggests that the gift of a "peace-weaver," a princess from one feuding race given in marriage to the prince of the enemy, does not end a feud if the people themselves do not accept the peace in their hearts--perhaps an early version of "cultural criticism." The opening story of Scyld not only defines a "good king," but also foreshadows Beowulf's career as a hero and king. The scop's song of Creation draws Grendel to Heorot, identifying him as the enemy of what is civilized, joyous, and creative; we see him as an agent of chaos and evil, and understand thereby the need for loyalty to God/god. Hrothgar's "sermon" or warning to Beowulf as he leaves Denmark for home reinforces the notion of how to be a good king; this speech, for Beowulf's benefit should he one day become king, tells how pride and greed lead to destruction and urges him that the diligent soul never sleeps in its efforts to hold off evil. Beowulf's retelling of his adventures is a little harder to account for in terms of its contribution to the poem as a whole. It may represent a leftover from the days of the oral delivery of the poem; if *Beowulf* was presented over more than a single sitting, an audience may have needed some reminder of what had passed in the narrative. It may also serve to illustrate the character of the hero: what he tells of his adventures and how he tells them. Perhaps it represents a ritual common in epic poetry: the hero's own recounting of his adventures (Odysseus does so, Gilgamesh returns home to do so, and Aeneas does so). The "Lay of the Last Survivor" (lines 2247-66) contributes to the elegiac tone of the whole epic and foreshadows not only Beowulf's death, but also the likely demise of his people following his death. Thus I think one may safely say that very little of *Beowulf* is wasted or pointless accretion.

⟡ The world of *Beowulf*--magical, heroic, transitory--though colored by the supernatural--magic swords, enchanted necklaces, dragons (according to the *Anglo-Saxon Chronicle*, some were spotted in the skies of Northumbria in the year 793)--never swerves too far from realism. *Lif is laene*, we learn: life is transitory. And even the greatest of monsters and heroes are mortal, waiting, perhaps courageously, for fate to catch up with them: *Gæth a wyrd swa hio scel*, fate ever goes as it must. Men must be loyal, brave, and generous, women must be pliant and patient in the face of tragedy, dragons must guard barrows full of treasure: their world defines them so and forces them to be so. Is that world Christian or pagan, since both Christian and Germanic worlds taught that one shouldn't cling to tightly to this little life? The poem contains three Judeo-Christian references, all from the Old Testament: Creation, the Great Flood, and the connection of Grendel to Cain. No reference to Christ or Christian doctrine or scripture appears--yet neither does any explicit mention of pagan gods. Pagan practices abound, in the funeral rites, for instance. We are also told that some of the Danes, after Grendel's attack, returned to their heathen sacrifices, that they "remembered hell in their heart-thoughts," that they did not "know the lord god"--a passage that sounds Christian, as does Hrothgar's "sermon" to Beowulf, laden with Patristic thinking. Yet the poet several times mentions the power of *wyrd* as a guiding force in the world, only to state in another passage that god watches over the world, as he always has. Even Beowulf suggests before his monster battles that the result rests in god's hands, though he adds: "Fate oft preserves the undoomed man if his courage holds." And Beowulf's sentiment following the death of Aeschere at the hands of Grendel's mother, "Better to avenge one's friend than to mourn overmuch," is a far cry from Christian thinking, resting instead in the the Germanic insistence on vengeance. The majority of scholars now believe that the *Beowulf* unites Christian and pagan-Germanic worlds, though some hold out for a "pagan poem by a Christian poet" or a "pagan poem doctored by a Christian redactor," or in a few instances, a Christian poem with "pagan coloring."

Despite this difficulty, we can discern several possible themes, sometimes depending on one's view of the poem as Christian or pagan, but sometimes independent of it. Advocates of "Christian" see in *Beowulf* an allegory or salvation, with Beowulf an example of the failure of paganism, since one's only immortality in the pagan world is in worldly fame, not Heaven, or with Beowulf as a Christ-type, the hero who sacrifices himself in the battle against evil and is deserted by his followers. Others see it as an exemplum of the dangers of pride or greed, since Beowulf seeks the glory of facing the dragon alone and for the sake of winning the hoard. Those who don't advocate a hard-line Christian reading see the fight with the dragon as something the hero-king must do: exhibiting his courage in defense of his people, avenging the dragon's attack, and continuing to earn *lof* and *dom*, fame and glory. Whether the poem be Christian or pagan, the ideal of steadfast courage applies.

The duality of *Beowulf* runs deeper yet: the poem has an apocalyptic feel, as though the poet intended to make a point about end-times, that they will come, are coming, and we must meet them. A final dragon battle occurs in both Christian and Norse apocalyptic stories: Michael's and Christ's with Satan in Revelation and Thor's with the World Serpent in the myth of Ragnarok. The Patristic virtues of *sapientia*, wisdom, and *fortitudo*, moral strength, also apply to the poem from either angle, as does *prudentia*, prudence (though to different effect in the two traditions), as Loren Gruber has recently suggested. It may also reflect the importance of loyalty or of community; it may suggest the opposition of indomitability vs. inevitability (Tolkien's thought); it may be simply an entertaining tale of marvels and monsters. One acute suggestion that I find students often make (partly following Schücking) is that it contrasts what makes a good king (courage, leadership, gift-giving, acquiring a strong army, having an heir) with what makes a good hero (courage, even bravado, achieving boasts, seeking adventures, boldness, even overboldness in combat)--the two don't always mix, and they require different responsibilities. But whether or not Beowulf makes the right decision in fighting the dragon, one must agree with Tolkien that he could hardly have found a more appropriate final adversary.

The complexity of the poem continues to yield many potential "meanings" without allowing readers to fix on any one with certainty.

Because of the debate over the date and provenance of *Beowulf*, scholars must be careful about suggesting sources of the poem, but several analogues appear for at least parts of the poem in addition to the couple I've already suggested. The Bear's Son folktale has obvious parallels, with its miraculous and mighty youth who kills monsters without weapons. Beo-wulf, bee-wolf, may himself have been suggested by a bear. The story of Sigemund and Fitela in the *Volsungasaga* parallels that of Beowulf and Wiglaf in some respects. Close analogues to Beowulf's battles with Grendel and Grendel's mother appear in Grettir's fights with Glamr and a she-troll in *Grettissaga*, and the character Bothvarr Bjarki in *Hrolfs Saga Kraka* also echoes that of Beowulf. Nearly all of the figures mentioned in *Beowulf* appear either in various Norse sagas or in sources of legend or history such as Saxo Grammaticus's *Gesta Danorum*. In fact, Beowulf himself may be the only figure in the poem not traceable to a historical person.

An excellent though early (98 A.D.) source for the structure of Germanic society is Tacitus' *Germania*, which describes the *comitatus* (*dryht* in Old English), headed by a lord with his band of retainers bound to him by an oath of loyalty to protect and fight for him in exchange for honor, gifts, and the mutual support of his soldiers. The comitatus appears not only in fact in *Beowulf*, but as a metaphor for Heaven or Hell throughout Old English poetry: support of one's lord leads to the dryht of Heaven, and failure of one's lord leads to the dryht of Hell (see Alvin Lee). Thus one may confidently say that *Beowulf* incorporates historical and poetic matter indicative of Germanic heroic and Christian heroic worlds. A Germanic-friendly reading might suggest that the poet was paying respects to the lost age of his or her ancestors, a Christian reading that the poem shows where the *comitatus* model failed. The world of the text does not allow an easy resolution, and thus *Beowulf* is a text ripe for discussion.

## THE OLD ENGLISH OF *BEOWULF*

I include here a brief sample, the first eleven lines, of the language and poetic style of *Beowulf* (drawn from the Wrenn-Bolton edition), followed by a brief analysis of its features.

> Hwæt wē Gār-Dena      in geār-dagum
> þēod-cyninga      þrym gefūnon,
> hū ða æthelingas      ellen fremedon.
>     Oft Scyld Scēfing      sceaþena þrēatum,
> monegum mægthum      meodo-setla oftēah;
> egsode Eorl[e],      syððan ærest wearth
> fēasceaft funden;      hē þæs frōfre gebād;
> wēox under wolcnum,      weorð-myndum þāh,
> oðþæt him æghwylc      þāra ymb-sittendra
> ofer hron-rāde      hyran scolde,
> gomban gyldan:      þæt was gōd cyning!

A word-for-word translation would sound like this:

> What? We of the spear-Danes in days of yore of the kings of
> the people the glories have heard, how the noble ones
> performed [deeds of] courage.  Often Scyld Scefing threatened
> many tribes of enemies, took [their] mead-benches, terrified
> men, since he first was found destitute.  He repaid that solace,
> grew under the skies, flourished with honor-memorials until
> him each of those dwelling round about over the whale road
> must heed, yield tribute:  that was a good king!

Notice the near repetition in the (probably stock) phrases "threatened enemies"
and "terrified men."  Notice also the hint of the supernatural in the very
beginning of the poem:  where did Scyld come from, and why did he arrive in
Denmark?  Fate?  God's plan?  The arrangement of the sample follows
traditional editorial practice with Old English verse.  The spacing between half-
lines does not appear in the manuscript, but represents an editorial convention
Also.  Further, the manuscript does not separate the poetic lines as we do in
modern verse, but carries each line to the edge of the page as though it were
prose.  Occasionally the manuscript will have a single dot indicating the end of
a poetic line or half-line.  Also, the manuscript has a few long-vowel marks; the
Wrenn-Bolton edition, from which the above sample is drawn, tries to
standardize the text by marking the long vowels similarly throughout the poem.
The student meeting Old English for the first time will also notice some
unfamiliar letters: þ, thorn, which has the "th" sound; ð, eth, which also has a
"th" sound; æ, asc (ash), which has the sound of the *a* in *that*.  Many readers
will immediately notice the similarity of Old English to German; it was a

version of Old Low German brought to England by the Angles ("Anglish"), Saxons, and Jutes in the fifth century. As for pronunciation, a few notes will help for the above sample. The vowels are like continental vowels, the *y* having the sound of the *u* in French *tu* or German *Tür*. An *e* at the end of a word sounds like a schwa. The indication of a long vowel means that one should hold it longer in speaking it; a doubled consonant means that one should make the sound twice: *siððan* is *sith-than*. Diphthongs stress the sound of the first vowel, the second reduced to the sound of the schwa. Consonants are like those in Modern English with a few exceptions: *c* is hard before or after a, o, and u, but has the sound of modern *ch* before or after i, e, or æ, and perhaps in final position in such words as *æghwylc*; *f* between two vowels sounds like modern *v*; *g* is hard before or after a, o, and u, but sounds like modern *y* before or after i, e, or æ; *h* at the end of a syllable sounds like the *ch* in German *ich*; *s* between two vowels sounds like modern *z*; *sc* sounds like modern *sh*. Stresses in the poetic line fall normally on alliterated syllables, but more strictly upon semantically stressed words and syllables (normally three or four per line).

While only a careful study of Old English leads to a full appreciation of the poem, *Beowulf* has too often been relegated to the desks of the philologists. It deserves the attention of all students interested in literature, and I hope that this volume will contribute to that end. Students interested in the art, history, or archeology of the time of the poem would do well to begin with these sources, detailed in the Selected Bibliography at the end of the book: Peter Hunter Blair, *An Introduction to Anglo-Saxon England*, David Wilson, *Anglo-Saxon Art*, Michael Wood, *In Search of the Dark Ages*, and M. O. H. Carver (editor), *The Age of Sutton Hoo*.

Students interested in the further study of *Beowulf* as a poem should also consult the bibliography. *Caveat*: those sources represent only the tip of the iceberg, those that I find most helpful to students working with the poem for the first time. Interested readers can find many more excellent sources that well may lead them to an unexpected love of what remains to us not only of *Beowulf*, but of a broad scope of artifacts and studies of the medieval world.

## GLOSSARY OF CHARACTERS

Abel, slain by his brother Cain in Genesis

Aelfhere, kinsman of Wiglaf

Aeschere, counselor of Hrothgar, killed by Grendel's mother

Beanstan, Breca's father

Beowulf the Dane, son of Scyld, later king of the Danes

Beowulf the Geat, hero of the Geats, later their king, slayer of
         Grendel, Grendel's mother, and the dragon

Breca, youth who had a rowing (some prefer "swimming") match with
         Beowulf

Brondings, the people of Beanstan and Breca

Brosings, makers of the magic necklace for the goddess Freya, probably a race
of fire-dwarfs in Germanic mythology

Cain, slayer of his brother Abel in Genesis

Daeghrafn, hero of the Hugas, slain by Beowulf during the battle in
         which Hygelac was slain

Eadgils, Swedish prince, son of Ohtere, brother of Eanmund

Eanmund, Swedish prince, son of Ohtere, brother of Eadgils

Ecglaf, father of Hunferth

Ecgtheow, father of Beowulf, of the kin of the Waegmundings

Ecgweala, a king of the Danes

Eofor, warrior of the Geats, slew Ongentheow

Eomer, son of Offa the Angle

Eormenric, a king of the Ostrogoths

Finn, a king of the East Frisians or Jutes

Fitela, nephew and battle-companion of Sigemund

Folcwalda, father of Finn

Freawaru, daughter of Hrothgar

Froda, a king of the Heathobards

Garmund, father of Offa the Angle

Gifthas, an east-Germanic tribe related to the Goths

Grendel, monstrous descendent of Cain, slain by Beowulf

Guthlaf, a Danish warrior

Haereth, father of Hygd, wife of Hygelac

Haethcyn, a son of Hrethel, a king of the Geats; older brother of Hygelac

Halga, a Danish prince, younger brother of Hrothgar

Hama, an earlier Germanic hero

Healfdane (Halfdane), a king of the Danes, father of Hrothgar

Heardred, son of Hygelac and Hygd, becomes king of Geatland, slain by
    Swedes
Heathobards, a Germanic tribe
Heatholaf, warrior slain by Ecgtheow, Beowulf's father
Heatho-Raemas, a Norwegian tribe
Helmings, family of Wealhtheow
Hemming, a kinsman of Offa the Angle
Hengest, a battle-leader of the Danes
Heorogar, a Danish king, elder brother of Hrothgar
Heorot, Hrothgar's mead-hall
Heoroweard, son of Heorogar the Dane
Herebeald, a Geatish prince, accidentally slain by his brother, Haethcyn
Heremod, a Danish king
Hereric, uncle of Heardred, probably brother of Hygd
Hetware, a Frankish tribe
Hildeburh, a Danish princess, married Finn
Hnaef, a prince of the Danes, brother of Hildeburh
Hoc, father of Hildeburh and Hnaef
Hondscio, a Geatish warrior, slain by Grendel
Hrethel, a king of the Geats, father of Hygelac
Hrethric, a son of Hrothgar and Wealhtheow
Hrothgar, king of the Danes, son of Healfdane
Hrothmund, a son of Hrothgar
Hrothulf, nephew of Hrothgar
Hugas, the Franks
Hunferth, a counselor of Hrothgar
Hunlafing, a retainer of Hengest
Hygd, queen of the Geats, wife of Hygelac
Hygelac, king of the Geats, Beowulf's lord
Ingeld, a prince of the Heathobards
Merewingas, the Franks
Modthrytho, wife of Offa the Angle
Offa, a king of the Angles
Ohtere, son of Ongentheow, king of the Swedes
Onela, a Swedish king, son of Ongentheow
Ongentheow, king of the Swedes
Oslaf, a Danish warrior
Scyldings, the Danes
Scyld Scefing, a Danish king, legendary founder of Hrothgar's family
Scylfings, the Swedes

Sigemund, legendary Norse dragonslayer
Swerting, an uncle of Hygelac
Vandals, a Germanic tribe
Waegmundings, family of Wiglaf, related to Beowulf
Waels, father of Sigemund
Wealhtheow, queen of the Danes, wife of Hrothgar
Weathers, the Geats
Weland, legendary Germanic smith and magician
Weohstan, father of Wiglaf
Wiglaf, kinsman of Beowulf and his appointed successor
Withergyld, a warrior of the Heathobards
Wonred, father of the Geatish warriors Eofor and Wulf
Wulf,  a Geatish warrior
Wulfgar, a prince of the Vandals
Wylfings, a Germanic tribe
Yrmenlaf, a Danish warrior, brother of Aeschere

# Beowulf

Hear!  We have heard        how in days past
the Spear-Danes,        princes of the peoples,
won glory,        did deeds of courage.
              Often Scyld Scefing        seized mead-benches
from the warrior bands        of many nations,
terrified noblemen,        since first he was found
possessing nothing--        he repaid that solace,
grew strong under heaven;        in fame he prospered
till every one        of the neighboring kingdoms
over the whale-road        had to heed him,
yield him tribute.        That was a good king!
              To them afterwards        was born a son,
young in the courtyards,        whom god sent
to comfort the countrymen.        He noted the suffering
that they had endured,        leaderless
a long while.        To him the lord of life,
guardian of glory,        gave worldly honors:
Beowulf was renowned,        Scyld's son,
his fame widespread        in Scandinavia.
Just so must a young man        bring about good          20
by gifts of treasure        to his father's followers,
so that after, in old age,        he may dwell with
willing comrades        and save the people
when war comes.        By generous deeds
one must prosper        in any nation.
              Scyld then left them        at the fated time,
still strong, to seek        the lord's succor.
They then carried him,        his loved companions,
to the sea's current,        just as he had asked,

when he still wielded words,      friend of the Scyldings,
the beloved land-leader      who had ruled so long.
There at the dock stood      the ring-prowed ship,
icy and eager,      the prince's vessel.
Then they laid down      their beloved lord
and giver of rings      in the ship's bosom
by the mast in mourning.      There was much treasure
from distant lands      and war-gear laden.
I have not heard      of a seemlier ship
adorned with armor      and weapons of war,
with blades and byrnies;      on his breast lay                    40
many treasures      that must fare with him
into the flood's grasp      far away.
Not at all was he less      provisioned with gifts,[1]
heirlooms of his people,      than they once did
who sent him at birth      far over the sea,
alone on the waves      when he was a child.
For him they placed      a golden standard
high over his head,      a gift for the warrior,
and let the sea bear him--      with sad hearts
they mourned his spirit.      Men do not know,
to say truly,      hall-counselors,
heroes under heaven,      who received that cargo.

      Then in the citadels      Beowulf of the Scyldings
was beloved king      for a long age,
famed among peoples,      his father gone elsewhere,
that prince of the land,      till to him was born
the great Healfdane,      who, fierce in battle,
ruled while he lived      the royal Scyldings.
From him in succession      came four children,
woke in the world      from the leader of armies,                    60
Heorogar and Hrothgar      and Halga the good;
I heard that Yrse      was Onela's queen,

---

[1]Here is an example of the *litotes* characteristic of Anglo-Saxon writing.

the battle-Scylfing's    beloved bed-companion.
      Then was Hrothgar given    victory in battle,
the fame of war    so that his kinsman
eagerly heeded him    till the youthful ones grew
into a great young army.    It came into his mind
that he would command    men to build
a hall-building,    a great mead-house
that the children of his age    would hear of forever
and within which    he would share everything
with young and old    of what god had given him,
except public land    and the lives of the people.
Then I have widely heard    work was ordered
from many peoples    throughout middle-earth
to adorn this folk-hall.    For him it befell
quickly among men    that it was finished,
greatest of halls:    he made the name "Heorot,"
he whose words had power    far and wide.
He broke no promise,    gave out rings                    80
and jewels at feasts.    The hall towered,
high and horn-gabled,    awaited the surging
of furious flames--    nor was it long then
till the sword-hate    of the oath-swearer
must arise    after malice.
      Then the bold demon    impatient with evil
suffered for a time,    he who waited in darkness,
as each day he    heard joy
build in the hall,    the sound of the harp,
sweet song of the scop.    He who knew told
of the making of men--    far back to relate!
He said the Almighty    made earth,
and the fair plain    that the water encircles.
He set triumphant    the sun and the moon
as lights to illuminate    earth's creatures,
and he decorated    earth's corners
with limbs and leaves.    He also made life,
each manner of thing    that lives and moves.

So the troop      lived in merriment
quite happily      until one began                          100
to commit crimes,      a fiend from hell.
That grim guest      was called Grendel,
great ghost of the marches      who ruled the wastelands,
fen and fastness,      land of the monster-folk.
The joyless man      watched awhile,
since the creator      had condemned him
as Cain's kin--      the eternal lord
avenged that murder      on him who slew Abel.
He did not joy in anger,      but the judge banished
him for his crime,      far away from mankind.
From Cain awoke      all the evil brood,
monsters and elves,      orcs and giants
such as those      who fought against god
a long age:      he paid them for that.
         He left then, Grendel,      when night had come,
to see the high hall,      how the Ring-Danes
after the beer-feast      bore themselves.
He found inside there      a troop of nobles
sleeping after the feast;      they knew no sorrow,
the misery of men.      The unholy creature,                120
grim and greedy,      soon was ready,
savage and cruel,      and from rest seized
thirty thanes;      then he left
rejoicing in plunder      to return home,
seek his lair      with the slain.
         Then with first light      at daybreak
Grendel's war-skill      was uncovered to men;
then after that feast      the sound of weeping arose,
a great morning-cry.      The famous lord,
that excellent prince,      sat sorrowful,
suffered gravely,      grieved for his thanes
after they examined      the enemy's track,
that of the accursed spirit.      That was trouble too great,
loathsome and long.      Nor was it longer

than after one night     he again committed
greater murder     and did not mourn for it,
from hatred and wickedness:     he was too fixed in such deeds.
Then it was easy to find     him who elsewhere,
farther away,     sought his resting place,
a bed in the aft-chambers,     when to him it was shown     140
and clearly told,     a manifest token
of the hall-warrior's hate.     He kept himself afterward
farther and safer,     he who escaped the fiend.
     So Grendel ruled     and fought against right,
one against all     until the best of halls
stood empty.     It was a great while,
a time of twelve winters     the lord of the Scyldings
grievously suffered     every woe,
the greatest of sorrows.     And so it was said
among the sons of men--     not dimly known--
in sad songs     that Grendel fought
long with Hrothgar,     showed fierce hatred,
the strife and feud     of many seasons,
continual struggle.     He did not wish peace
with any man     of the troop of the Danes,
to quit the slaughter     and settle for tribute;
nor did any of the councilors     need to expect
bright payment     from the slayer's hands.
But the monster     was pursuing--
dark death-shadow--     veterans and youth;     160
he hovered and lurked     till perpetual night ruled
the misty moors.     Men did not know
whither he wandered,     who knew hell's secrets.
     Thus many evils     the enemy of mankind,
monstrous lone-stalker     often committed,
worse humiliations.     By Heorot he dwelt,
the jewel-adorned hall,     in the black nights.
He could not approach     the gift-seat,
treasure before god--     he did not know his love.
That was great misery     to the lord of the Scyldings,

a grief of the spirit.       Many often sat,
nobles at council,       considered advice,
what were best       for the brave ones
to do against       the sudden-horror.
Sometimes they sacrificed       at the temples of idols,
doing them honor,       prayed in words
that the soul-slayer       send help
against the nation-scourge.       Such was their practice,
custom of heathens.       They remembered hell
in their heart-thoughts;       they did not know the measurer,  180
judge of deeds,       nor know the lord god,
nor know how to praise       the protector of heavens,
ruler of the world.       Woe be to those
who through dire ill       thrust the soul
into the fire's embrace,       expect no comfort,
by any means change.       Well is it for those who may
after their death-day       seek out the lord
and ask peace       in the father's embrace.
　　　So on the sorrow of the time       the son of Healfdane
continually brooded,       nor could the wise warrior
turn aside his woes:       that sorrow was too strong,
loathsome and long,       which had come on the people,
grim violence,       worst of night-terrors.
　　　Thus from home heard       Hygelac's thane,
good man of the Geats,       of Grendel's deeds;
he was of mankind       the greatest in might
in those days       of this life,
noble and mighty.       He ordered prepared
a wave-traveler;       he said he would seek
over the swan-road       the warrior-king,                              200
the great lord,       who needed men.
With that adventure       wise men
found little fault,       though he was dear to them.
they urged on the valiant one,       examined the omens.
From the people of the Geats       the good man
chose champions,       the best of those

he could find--    they were fifteen in all--
and sought the sea-wood.      The warrior led them,
the sea-skilled man,      to the land-boundary.
          A time passed;      a floater was on the waves,
a craft under the cliffs.      Ready soldiers
climbed into the prow;      currents eddied,
swimming along the shore.      The warriors carried
into the bosom of the ship      bright weapons
and noble battle-armor.      The men shoved off
on a longed-for adventure      in the well-braced ship,
embarked over the wave-way      urged by the wind,
the foamy-necked floater      most like a bird,
till after a due time      the next day
the curve-prowed ship      had advanced                          220
so that the seafarers      saw land,
the sea-cliffs gleam,      the steep shores,
the wide sea-headlands.      Then was ocean traversed,
the voyage at an end.      Then up quickly
"the people of the weather"      ascended the plain,
tied up their ship.      The mail-shirts clanked,
garments of war.      They thanked god
that the sea-trek      had gone easily for them.
          Then from the wall      the Scyldings' watchman,
he who must guard      the sea-cliffs,
saw them tote over the gangway      bright shields,
ready war-gear.      Curiosity pressed him
in his heart-thoughts      who the men were.
He went then to the shore,      Hrothgar's thane,
rode his horse,      nobly brandished
the mighty spear in his hands,      in formal speech asked:
          "What are you,      armored ones,
protected with byrnies,      who thus in a tall ship
over the water-road      have come on a journey
over the sea?      I for a time have been                          240
a coast-guard,      have held sea-watch
so that in the land of the Danes      no enemies

by ship-force      could harm us.
Not more openly      have shield-bearers
undertaken to come,      nor were you certain
you would have formal leave      of our warriors,
the consent of kinsmen.      Never have I seen greater man
among the nobles of earth      than is one of you,
a warrior in armor;      nor is that a "hall soldier,"
honored by weapons.      Never may appearance belie him,
his matchless demeanor.      Now I must
learn your lineage      lest you go hence
as deceiving spies,      fare farther
into the land of the Danes.      Now you far-dwellers,
seafarers      hear my
plain thought:      Quickest is best
to make known      whence you are come."
          The senior man      answered him,
leader of the troop,      unlocked his word-hord:
"We are men      of the nation of the Geats                    260
and Hygelac's      hearth-companions.
My father was      well-known among peoples,
a noble battle-front leader      called Ecgtheow.
He lived a great many winters      before he passed away,
old in the courtyards;      every wise man
widely throughout the earth      certainly remembers him.
With friendly heart we      have come to seek
your lord,      the son of Healfdane,
protector of the people--      Be of good counsel to us!
We have a great mission      to the famous one,
lord of the Danes,      nor must anything be secret,
I think.      You know if it is
truly as we      have heard said,
that among the Scyldings      an ememy--I don't know what--
a mysterious persecutor      in the dark nights
manifests through terror      an unknown hatred
humiliation and slaughter.      I can teach Hrothgar,
with open-mindedness,      a plan in this matter,

how he, wise and good,    can overcome the fiend,
if for him a change    may ever come,                    280
a remedy in turn,    so the affliction of griefs,
the surging of sorrows    become cooler,
else ever after    he endures great hardship,
an age of distress,    while there remains
in a high place    the best of halls."
         The watchman spoke,    sat there on the horse,
fearless officer:    "Each must
a keen shield-warrior    determine to know:
words and deeds--    he who thinks well.
I find    that this is a troop true
to the lord of the Scyldings.    Go forth and bear
weapons and gear.    I will lead you.
And I will command    my young retainers
against any enemies    to guard with honor
your craft    newly tarred,
ship on the sand,    until again it bears
friendly men    over the sea-currents,
the curve-necked wood    to the Weather's shore
with the ones who act bravely,    and if it be given
that he survive whole    the onrush of battle.            300
         They then turned to go;    the ship remained still,
the broad-breasted ship    rode on hawsers,
fast at anchor.    Boar-figures shone
over cheek-protectors    adorned with gold,
blood-bright and fire-hardened    stood guard over lives
of fierce battle-ready ones.    The men hurried,
marched together    until they could see
the timbered hall,    noble and gold-bright,
which was foremost    among earth-folk
of buildings under the skies,    in which the king lived:
that light shone    over many lands.
To them the battle-bold one    the bright house
of the brave ones pointed out    so they could go
directly to it.    A certain one of the warriors

turned his horse      and then spoke a word:
"It is time for me to go;      the father all-powerful
guard you      with kindness,
safe in ventures.      I will go the the sea
to keep watch      against enemy troops.
•      The street was stone-paved,      the way determined      320
for the men together.      War-mail shone,
hard, hand-linked,      bright iron-rings
sung in the armor.      When they had just
come to the hall      in their grim armor,
the sea-weary ones set      wide shields,
magically hard bosses      against the wall of the hall,
and sat down then on benches--      mail-shirts rung,
battle-armor of men.      Spears stood,
gear of seaman,      together also,
an ash-holt with gray tops:      the iron-clad troop
was honored in weapons.      There a proud hero
nobly asked      the sword-wielders:
"Whence do you travel,      you of the gold-plated shields
gray mail-shirts      and grim-helmets,
a company of battle-spears?      I am Hrothgar's
herald and officer.      I have not seen among foreigners
this many men      of bolder heart.
I expect that out of daring--      not at all from exile--
but from greatness of heart      you have sought Hrothgar."
        Then the valor-famed one      answered him,      340
brave leader of the Weathers      hardy under helm
spoke a word in turn:      "We are Hygelac's
board-companions;      Beowulf is my name.
I want to proclaim      to the son of Healfdane,
famous lord,      my errand
to your prince,      if he, the good one,
wishes to grant us      that we may greet him."
        Wulfgar answered,      who was of the Vandals--
his spirit      was known to many
for boldness and wisdom--      "I will ask

the leader of the Danes,      lord of the Scyldings,
giver of rings,      famous ruler,
as you are a petitioner,      about your venture,
and what the answer is      I will quickly make known,
what reply the good one      thinks to give back."
          He then turned quickly      to where Hrothgar sat,
old and gray,      with his troop of nobles.
The famed one went      so he stood shoulder-to-shoulder
with the lord of the Danes:      he knew noble custom.
Wulfgar formally addressed      his friend and lord:          360
"A troop is arrived,      come from afar
over the span of sea      from the nation of the Geats;
the senior      of the sword-wielders
is named Beowulf.  They are boon-seekers,
my lord,      that they might
exchange words with you.      Refuse them
no reply,      gracious Hrothgar;
in war-gear      they seem worthy
of the esteem of men.      Truly the senior has might,
he who hither      led the warriors."
          Hrothgar answered,      protector of Scyldings,
"I knew him      when he was a boy;
his father      was called Ecgtheow,
who for his home gave      Hrethel of the Geats
his only daughter.      It is his son now,
strong, has come here,      sought out a loyal friend.
Then it was said      by seafarers,
those who brought      tribute from the Geats
thither to offer thanks,      that he had
in his hand-grip      the strength of thirty men          380
brave in battle.      Holy god
out of kindness      has sent him to us,
to the West-Danes,      so that I may have hope
against Grendel's terror.      To that good man
for his heart's-courage      I must offer treasures.
Be in haste:      command those kinsmen

to come in    together to see me;
say to them also    that they are welcome
among the folk of the Danes."    Then Wulfgar went
to the doors of the hall    and announced from inside,"
"I am commanded to tell you    by my victory-lord,
elder of the East-Danes,    that he knows your lineage
and that over the sea-billows,    bold in mind,
you are to him    welcome here.
Now you may go    in your battle-armor,
under your war-masks,    to see Hrothgar.
Let battle-shields    and deadly spear-shafts
await here    the result of words."
      The noble one arose,    many men about him,
a mighty group of thanes.    Some stayed there        400
to guard the battle-armor    as the brave one bade them.
Hastening together    the warriors were guided
under Heorot's roof.    The battle-bold one,
hard-under-helm,    advanced so he stood inside the hall.
      Beowulf spoke--    his mail-coat shone,
      the armor-net sewn    by the skill of a smith--
"Be healthy, Hrothgar;    I am Hygelac's
kinsman and young retainer.    I have undertaken in youth
many glorious deeds.    The matter of Grendel
became openly known    to me in my homeland.
The seafarers say    that this hall stands,
best of buildings,    idle and useless
to each of its warriors    after evening light
is held concealed    under heaven's firmament.
Then my people    instructed me,
the best    of the wise men,
Lord Hrothgar,    because they knew
my military skill,    so that I sought you out.
They themselves looked on    when I came from battle,
blood-stainded from enemies,    where I bound five,      420
destroyed a tribe of giants,    and slew in the waves
at night water demons,    endured narrow rations,

avenged the Weathers' affliction--     woes they sought--
obliterated fierce foes;       and now alone
against Grendel      I shall undertake
a meeting with the monster.      I now
want to ask,      prince of the bright-Danes,
shelterer of Scyldings,       one boon,
that you not refuse me,       protector of warriors,
dear friend of the people,       now that I have come so far,
that I might alone,      with my company of nobles,
this troop of hardy ones,       cleanse Heorot.
I have found by asking       that the monster
in his recklessness       does not care for weapons.
I then forgo them,      so my liege-lord,
Hygelac, will be      pleased of heart,
that I bear a sword      and a broad shield,
yellow linden-wood to war,      but I with my hand grip
shall battle the fiend      and fight over life,
enemy against enemy:       there must he trust                      440
in god's judgment,      he whom death takes.
I expect he will wish,       if he can manage
in the war-hall,      to eat fearlessly
of the Geatish people      as he has often done
strong glory-warriors.       You will not need
to hide my head,      but he will want to have me,
shining with flowing blood,       if death takes me,
will carry the bloody corpse,       intend to taste--
the lone-walker will eat      without regret,
stain his wasteland-lair.       You will have no need
to be anxious long      about my body's disposal.
If battle takes me,      send to Hygelac
the best of mail-coats,      which my breast wears,
finest of garments;       it is Hrethel's inheritance,
the work of Weland.      Fate ever goes as it must!"
          Hrothgar spoke,      protector of Scyldings:
"My friend Beowulf,      to defend us in battle
and for honor      you sought us;

your father struck     the gravest of blows
when he became the hand-slayer     of Heatholaf     460
among the Wylfings.     Then the people of the Weathers
could not keep him     because of their fear of war.
Thence he sought     the South-Danish folk,
the honor-Scyldings,     over the rolling waves;
then I first ruled     the Danish people
and in youth held     the gem-kingdom,
treasure-stronghold of heroes.     Heorogar was dead,
my older kinsman     no longer living,
son of Healfdane:     he was better than I.
Afterwards I settled     the feud with payment.
I sent to the Wylfings     ancient treasurers
over the water's ridge;     he swore oaths to me.[2]
It is a sorrow to me     in my heart to say
to any man     what Grendel has done to me,
injury on Heorot     with his thoughts of hate
and his attacks.     My hall-troop,
warrior-band is lessened;     fate swept them off
in Grendel's horror.     God can easily put
the rash ravager's     deeds to an end.
Full often     warriors boasted
over ale-cups,     drunk with beer,     480
that in the beer-hall     they wished to await
Grendel's attack     with the terror of swords;
Then was the mead-hall     in morning time,
the noble place blood-stained     when day gleamed,
all the bench-planks     drenched with blood,
the hall with battle-gore.     I had fewer loyal ones,
dear veterans,     for those whom death took away.
For now sit at feast     and attend in joy
to the victories of glory-soldiers     as your heart desires.

---

[2]Hrothgar paid Ecgtheow's *weregild*, and Ecgtheow swore an oath of loyalty to Hrothgar.

> Then a bench was cleared        in the beer-hall
> for the men of the Geats        all together.
> There the stout-hearted ones        went to sit,
> proud in their strength.        A thane attended to his office,
> he who in his hands bore        adorned ale-cups
> and poured out bright drink.        Sometimes the scop sang
> clearly in Heorot;        there was the merriment of heroes,
> no few veteran warriors        of Danes and Weathers.
>         Hunferth spoke,        Ecglaf's son,
> who sat at the feet        of the lord of the Scyldings,        500
> unbound a battle-rune;        Beowulf's venture,
> the courage of the seafarer,        was to him great vexation
> because he did not deem        that any other man
> in middle-earth        under the heavens
> accomplished more        than he himself:
> "Are you that Beowulf        who contended against Breca,[3]
> had a contest in rowing        in the broad sea,
> where you two for pride        tested the ocean
> and because of foolish boasting        risked your lives
> in the deep water?        Nor could any man,
> neither friend nor foe,        dissuade you two
> from the grievous venture        when you rowed into the sea.
> There with your arms        you enfolded the current,
> measured the sea-paths,        swung with your hands,
> glided over wind's-edge.        The sea surged in waves
> in winter's wellings.        In possession of the water
> you labored seven nights.        He beat you at rowing,
> had the greater strength.        Then in the morning-tide
> among the Heatho-Raemas        the sea carried him up.
> Thence he sought        his own dear native land        520

---

[3]The insult-match between Hunferth and Beowulf may constitute a northern Germanic ritual. Also, scholars have argued over whether Beowulf and Breca had a rowing match of a swimming match. And though most editors and translators use the spelling *Unferð*, the ms. reads *Hunferð*.

beloved by his people,      land of the Brondings,
fair citadel,      where he ruled kin,
stronghold, and treasures.      All his vow against you
the son of Beanstan      truly performed.
Thus I expect of you      worse results,
though in the onrush of battle      you were always doughty,
wrathful in war,      if you dare
for a whole night      wait nearby for Grendel.
          Beowulf spoke,      Ecgtheow's son:
"Indeed you say a great amount      about Breca,
my friend Hunferth,      drunk with beer,
about his exploits.      The truth I tell
is that I had greater      sea-strength,
hardships in the waves,      than any other man.
We said that,      when we two were boys
and boasted,      both then still
in the time of youth,      that we would risk our lives
out in the wind's edge,      and we accomplished it so.
We had naked swords,      when we rowed in the current,
fast in our hands--      we thought to protect ourselves      540
against whales.      Nor could he by any means
float farther      from me in the flood-waves,
more quickly in the sea,      nor did I wish to from him.
Then we two together      were in the sea
a period of five nights,      until the flood drove us apart,
the surging sea,      the coldest of weather,
the darkening night,      and the north wind,
battle-fierce, turned against us.      Rough were the waves,
and the temper of the sea-fish      was roused.
There against enemies      my body-mail,
hard and hand-linked,      woven battle-shirt,
provided me help,      lay on my breast
adorned with gold.      A hostile ravager
drew me to the bottom,      tightly had me
grimly in his grip;      however it was granted to me
that I with the point      of my battle-sword

reached the monster--      the rush of battle took
the mighty water-beast      by means of my hand.
So often      loathed despoilers
threatened me direly.      I served them                     560
with my dear sword,      as it was fitting.
Nor did they have there      a feast to rejoice in,
evil-doers,      in which they partook of me,
sat round at feast      on the sea-floor.
But in the morning      with sword-wounds
they lay up      along the wave-leavings,
put to sleep by my sword,      so that afterwards
they never hindered      seafarers journeys
across the steep water.      Light came from the east,
god's bright beacon,      and the seas stilled,
so that I could see      the sea-headlands,
the windy walls.      Fate oft preserves
the undoomed man      if his courage holds.
However, to me it was given      that with sword I slew
nine water-demons.      I have never heard in the night
under the vault of heaven      of a harder fight,
nor of a harder-beset man      in the water-currents.
However:  I survived far back      the grasp of hostile ones,
weary from the venture.      Then the sea bore me up,
flood after the current,      the water welling,              580
onto the land of the Lapps.      Never have I heard spoken
anything with respect to you      of such battles,
of the terror of swords.      Breca never yet,
neither of you two,      performed deeds
so bravely      at battle-play
with blood-stained swords,      nor do I boast much of that,
though you were the slayer      of your brother,
near-kinsman--      for that in hell you must
endure damnation,      though your wit be good.
I say to you truly,      son of Ecglaf,
that Grendel had never done      so much horror,
terrible monster,      against your leader,

humiliation in Heorot,      if your heart
were as fierce in battle      as you claim.
But he has found      he need not fear
very much the feud      awful sword-storm,
with your folk,      the Victory-Scyldings.
He takes his tribute,      having no mercy,
from the nation of the Danes,      but displays his delight,
slays and dispatches,      does not expect battle                    600
from the spear-Danes.      But I shall show him
quite soon now      the strength and spirit
of the Geats in battle.      He who can will again go,
brave one, to his mead      after the morning light
of another day,      the sun clothed in radiance,
shines from the south      over the children of men."

        Then was he joyful,      the giver of jewels,
gray-haired and war-famous;      the chief of the bright-Danes
expected help,      counted on Beowulf,
guardian of the people,      resolved in thought.
There was heroes' laughter--      it made a pleasing ring--
and their words were winsome.      Wealhtheow came forward,
Hrothgar's queen,      mindful of manners.
She greeted the gold-adorned      men in the hall,
and then the noble lady      passed a full cup
to the first of the east-Danes,      guardian of the land;
she bade him be glad      at the beer-drinking.
Beloved of his people,      he received with pleasure
feast and hall-cup,      victory-famed king.
Round then went      the lady of the Helmings                    620
to veterans and to youth,      a portion into each
of the precious cups poured      until the time came to pass
that the ring-adorned queen,      excelling in spirit,
carried the mead-cup      to Beowulf.
She greeted the leader of the Geats,      thanked god
wisely in words      that her wish had come to pass,
that she in any man      might hope for
comfort for crimes.      He received that cup,

fierce battle-warrior,      from Wealhtheow,
and then made a speech,      made ready for battle;
         Beowulf spoke,      Ecgtheow's son:
"I resolved it,      when I set out to sea,
sat down in the sea-craft      with my band of men,
that I will completely      achieve the wish
of your people      or fall in slaughter
fast in the fiend's grip.      I shall perform
worthy acts of courage      or experience
my last day      in the mead-hall.
The woman liked well      those words,
the boast of the Geat.      She went, gold-adorned,            640
noble queen of her people,      to sit by her lord.
         Then it was again as before      inside the hall,
mighty-words spoken,      the nation joyful,
the sound of victory-folk      until presently
the son of Healfdane      wished to seek
a night's rest;      since he could see
the sun's light      he knew the monster
awaited battle      on the high-hall
until the darkening      night had come
to glide over all      of the shapes of the shadows
wan under the skies.      The troop all arose.
Then one of the men,      Hrothgar, saluted
the other, Beowulf,      wished him health,
control of the wine-hall,      and spoke this speech:
"Since I could raise      hand and shield,
never before      have I entrusted to any man
the mighty hall of the Danes,      except now to you.
Hold now and guard      the best of houses,
remember glory,      well-known deeds of valor;
keep watch against the enemy.      Nor will you lack anything  660
you wish if you survive      that courage-work."
     Then Hrothgar departed      from the hall
with his band of men,      protector of the Scyldings;
the war-leader wished      to seek Wealhtheow,

to go to bed with the queen.      The glory-king had,
as men have learned,       set a hall-guardian
against Grendel.       He took up this duty
for the elder of the Danes,       offered giant-watch.
Truly the prince of the Geats      readily trusted
in his brave might      and the measurer's grace.
Then he took off      his iron corselet
and the helmet from his head,      gave his decorated sword
of the choicest iron      to an attendant
and commanded that      the war-gear be guarded.
The good man then spoke,      Beowulf of the Geats,
a certain word of boasting,      before he stepped into bed:
"Not at all in my war-vigor      and my battle-deeds
do I consider them poorer      than Grendel does his;
therefore I will not      slay him with sword,
deprive him of life so,      though I easily could.        680
He does not know their virtue,      so that he might hew
a shield to pieces,      though he be famed
in deeds of violence,      but we two tonight shall
forgo the use of swords,      if he dare to seek
battle without a weapon,      and thereupon wise god,
the holy lord,      deem glory
on whichever hand      he finds it fitting."
          The battle-brave one reclined;      the noble's face
took a cheek-cushion,      and around him many
bold seamen      lay down to hall-rest.
None of them thought      that he from there would
ever again seek      his beloved homeland,
the folk and noble-fortress      where he was fed.
But they had learned      that before them murder
had taken too many of the great ones      in the wine-hall
from the Danish people;      but to them the lord gave
the fate of war-victory,      comfort and help
to the people of the weathers,      that they entirely
overcame their enemy      through one man's skill,
by his own might.      The truth is known,        700

that mighty god      rules always
the race of men.      In the dark night came
striding a walker-in-shadows;      the bowmen slept,
those who were supposed to guard      the horn-gabled hall,
all except one.      It was known to men
that the evil enemy      could not,
when god did not wish it,      draw them under the shadows,
but he was watching      in anger for his foes,
awaited heart-swollen      the result of battle.
          Then from the moor      under the mist-slopes
came Grendel walking--      he bore god's wrath.
The evil-doer intended      to ensnare one
of the race of men      in the high hall,
advanced under the skies      until he most readily recognized
the wine-hall,      the gold-hall of men,
with gold-plates shining.      Nor was that the first journey
that he had sought      to Hrothgar's home;
Never in his life-days      neither before nor since
did he find with harder fortune      a hall-thane.
He came then to the hall,      the warrior venturing,      720
deprived of joys.      The door, fast with fire-forged bands,
at once gave way      when he touched it with his hands.
The bale-planning one swung open      the door of the hall
when he was enraged.      Quickly then after
the fiend trod      on the shining floor,
went wrathfully--      from his eyes stood out,
most like flame,      a foul light.
He saw in the hall      many soldiers,
a sleeping band of kinsman      all together,
a troop of young warriors.      Then his heart laughed;
the horrible monster      intended that before morning
he part      each one of them
life from body      when he expected
his fill of feasting.      But it was not his fate
that after that night      he was ever again to consume
more of the race of men.      The mighty one waited,

kinsman of Hygelac,      to see how the wicked ravager
under the sudden grip of attack      intended to proceed.
Nor was it that the monster      intended to delay,
but he quickly seized      at first opportunity              740
a sleeping soldier      and tore him without hindrance,
bit into the joints,      drank the blood at once,
swallowed in sinful bites.      Soon he had
entirely consumed      the unliving one,
feet and hands.      Forward nearby he stepped,
seized with his hands      the stronghearted one,
the soldier in bed--      the enemy reached out
with his hands.      Beowulf quickly grasped him
with hostile intent      and sat up on his arm.
Soon the keeper-of-crimes      discovered that
he had not met      in middle-earth
in this region of the world      among other men
a greater hand-grip.      He became in his courage
fearful in spirit;      none the quicker could he get away.
The heart in him eagerly wished      to flee into the darkness
to seek the company of devils.      His lot there was not
such as in elder-days he      had ever met.
Then the good man remembered,      kinsman of Hygelac,
his evening-speech,      stood upright
and tightly took hold of him;      fingers strained--              760
the giant was trying to escape.      The man stepped further.
The notorious intended,      such as he could,
to turn wider      and on his way thence
to flee to his fen-retreat,      knew the fingers' power
in the fierce one's grasp.      That was a sadder venture
that the harmful-foe      took to Heorot.
          The troop-hall resounded.      Among all of the Danes,
the fortress-dwellers,      each one of the braver men,

there were ale-showers.        Wrathful were both,[4]
fierce house-guardians.      The hall echoed:
it was a great wonder        that the wine-hall held
against brave-in-battle ones,       that the fair earth-hearth
did not fall to the ground.      But it was so firm
inside and out        with iron bands
skillfully smithed.      There fell away on the floor
many mead-benches,        as I have heard,
gold-adorned,        where the fierce ones fought.
Scylding wise men        did not expect this before,
that any one of humankind        ever by any means
could shatter it,      splendid and antler-adorned,                 780
by cunning destroy it,        unless the embrace of flames
swallowed it in fire.      Noise lept up
anew often;       the north-Danes stood
in dreadful terror,        each one
of them who from the wall        heard weeping,
a terrible song to sing,        from god's enemy
a victory-less song        to bewail his defeat,
captive of hell.      He held him fast,
he who of men        was the strongest in might
in those days        of this life.
Nor would the protector of men        by any means
leave alive        the murderous-visitor,
nor did any of the men        consider useful
his life-days.      There most often
Beowulf's men        drew old swords;
they wished to defend        their lord's life,
the fame of the leader        as best they could.
They did not know,        when they drew into the fray,
stern-minded        sword-soldiers,

---

[4]The word *ealu-scerwen* has drawn much critical attention. See, recently, Stephen O. Glosecki's "*Beowulf* 769:   Grendel's Ale-Share," in *English Language Notes* 25.1, 1987, 1-9.

and on every side      thought to hew,                          800
to seek the life      of the evil-enemy,
that throughout earth none      of the best of swords,
none of the battle-blades      would touch him,
but victory-weapons he      had made useless by magic,
any sword.      It had to be that his death
in those days      of this life
be miserable      and the alien-spirit
in the power of fiends      to travel far.
          Then he discovered,      he who before many
crimes committed      against the race of men
to spirits' sorrow--      he fought against god--
that his body      would not serve,
but the mighty one,      kinsman of Hygelac,
had him in his hands;      each to the other was,
living, loathsome.      The horrible monster
suffered a body-wound:      in his shoulder was
manifest a sin-payment;      sinews sprung out,
joints burst.      To Beowulf was given
glory in battle.      Grendel had to flee
from there life-sick      under the fen-slope            820
to seek a joyless dwelling;      he knew the more surely
that his life was      come to an end,
the number of his days.      After that battle-storm
the wish of all the Danes      was come to pass.
He who had come from afar,      wise and stout-hearted,
had then purged      Hrothgar's hall, had
protected against attack.      He rejoiced in the night-work,
in heroic deeds.      To the east-Danes
the leader of the Geatmen      had carried out his boast,
completely remedied      such grief,
malice-sorrow,      as they had experienced before
and out of dire necessity      had to suffer,
no small affliction.      That was a clear token,
since the battle-brave one      laid down the hand,
arm and shoulder--      there altogether was

Grendel's claw      under the vaulted roof.
         Then in the morning      I have heard
around the gift-hall      were many warriors.
The leaders of the people      far and near
throughout the wide-regions      beheld the wonder,          840
the loathed one's tracks.      His parting from life
seemed not at all grievous      to any of the men
who beheld the footprints      of the inglorious one,
how the weary spirit      on the way thence,
overcome in battle,      bore his life-tracks
into the lake of water-demons,      doomed and put to flight.
There the water was      boiling with blood,
violent surging of waves      all mingled
with hot gore,      welled up with battle-blood.
The death-fated one hid,      since joyless
in the fen-refuge      he laid his life,
heathen soul:      there hell received him.
         The old companions      thence again departed,
also many young ones      from the joyful journey,
rode on their mares      brave from the lake,
heroes on horses.      There Beowulf's
glorious deed was proclaimed;      many often said
that south or north      between the two seas,
over the whole vast earth      none other
under the expanse of heaven      was ever a better          860
shield-bearer,      more worthy of a kingdom.
Nor did they truly find fault      with the friend-lord,
gracious Hrothgar,      but that he was a good king.
         Meantime brave-in-battle ones      were allowed to leap,
to ride in races      of the yellow mares
where the earth-road      seemed fair to them
and were best known.      Sometimes the king's thane,
a speech-laden man      mindful of tales,
he who of the great number      of the ancient tales
remembered many,      found other words
aptly linked.      The man in turn began

skillfully to recite      Beowulf's exploit
and successfully to compose      a ready story,
to turn it into words.      He told of everything
that he had heard said      about Sigemund,
of deeds of courage,      of many uncanny things,
of the Waelsing's strife,      of far journeys,
of matters the children of men      did not know fully,
of feuds and crimes--      except Fitela with him,
when he wished to say      something truly                    880
uncle to his nephew,      since they were ever
companions-at-need      to each other in trouble.
They slew with swords      very many
of the race of giants.      Sigemund's fame
spread not a little      after his death-day,
since hardened by war      he killed a dragon,
keeper of treasure.      Under a gray stone he,
son of a prince      alone risked
the audacious deed,      nor was Fitela with him;
but to him it was given      that that sword penetrated
the wondrous worm,      that it stood fixed in the body wall,
lordly iron--      the dragon had died by murder.
The terrifying one had      gone with courage[5]
so that he could enjoy      the treasure-hord
at his own will;      the sea-boat he loaded,
bore bright treasures      in the hold of the ship,
the son of Waels.      The worm had melted in the heat.
          He was the hero      most widely famous
across the race of men,      protector of warriors,
for deeds of courage      (he had prospered for that before)   900
since Heremod's      war-valor diminished,
his strength and courage.      He among a monstrous folk
was betrayed      into the power of enemies,

---

[5]The poet applies the word *aglæca* to both monsters and heroes, including both Grendel and Beowulf. I translate it as "terrifying one."

speedily sent to death.        Concerning him, sorrow-surgings
troubled too long--      he was to his people,
to all his nobles,        too great a life-grief.
So in former times        many a wise man
often grieved over        the stout-hearted one's departure,
he who trusted in him        for a remedy for evils,
that that lord's son        should prosper,
receive the father's rank,        protect the people,
treasure and citadel,        kingdom of heroes,
the homeland of Scyldings.        There he was to all,
the kinsman of Hygelac,        to friends the most pleasing
of the race of men.        Crime took possession of Heremod.
          ❧ Sometimes contending        on the yellow tracks,
They travelled on horses.        Then the morning light was
shoved on and hastened.        Many a retainer went
strong-minded        to the hall of the high one
to see the strange wonder.        Also the king himself,        920
guardian of the treasure-hoard,        from the woman's bower
trod the famous-one        with his great troop
known for excellence,        and his queen with him stepped
on the path to the mead-hall        with a host of women.
          Hrothgar spoke--        he went to the hall,
stood on the step,        beheld the high rood
shining with gold        and Grendel's hand:
"For this sight        make swiftly
thanks to the all-powerful one;        I bore many loathsome
griefs from Grendel.        God can ever work
wonder after wonder,        shepherd of glory.
It was just lately        that I for myself
in a long life        did not expect to live
to see a remedy        when, stained with blood,
the best of houses        stood dripping battle-gore,
widespread woe        among all the wise ones,
of those who did not think        that they for a long-life
would protect the people's earth-work        from enemies,
devils and demons.        Now a retainer,

through the lord's might,      has done the deed          940
that we all      could not before
skillfully contrive.      Truly one can say it,
that even that same woman      who begot that son
after the race of men,      if she yet lives,
that to her the ancient-creator      was gracious
in child-bearing.      Now you, Beowulf,
best of warriors,      I will love you in life
like a son;      keep well henceforth
the new kinship.      Nor will you lack anything
of the world that you wish      over which I have power.
Very often I have assigned      reward for less,
treasure-honors      to poorer warriors
inferior at battle.      You yourself have
performed deeds      so that your fame will live
for ever and ever.      The all-wielder
reward you well,      as he has done thus far."
         Beowulf spoke,      Ecgtheow's son:
"With great favor      we fought to perform
that courage-work,      daringly risked
against unknown strength.      I would much rather          960
that you yourself      could have seen him,
the fiend in his glory      death-weary.
I quickly      clasped him tightly,
in a death-bed      thought to bind him,
so because of my hand-grip      he must
lie straining for life,      unless his body escape.
The measurer did not wish it--      I could not
hinder him from going,      though I so eagerly held on
to the mortal-foe;      the fiend in flight
was too powerful.      However, he left his hand
to save his life;      arm and shoulder
remain behind.      Nor there, though, did
the destitute one      buy any comfort;
no longer will he live,      loathsome-spoiler,
for his sins struck down,      but pain had him

in its compulsive grip,      closely seized,
baleful one in bonds.      There must he wait,
the guilt-stained man,      for the great judgment,
how the bright measurer      will wish to decree."
      Then the man was quieter,      the son of Ecglaf,      980
in boast-speech      of battle-works
after the nobles--      by the man's skill--
up towards the high roof      examined the hand,
the fingers of the fiend.      At the tip was,
in place of each nail,      most like steel,
the heathen's hand-talon,      the battle-warrior's
ungentle spike.      Each man asserted that,
of harder things,      none would damage it,
ever-good iron,      such that the terrifying one's
bloody battle-hand      would weaken.
      Then it was quickly commanded      the inside of Heorot
be decorated by hands;      many men
and women were there,      those who adorned the wine-hall,
the guest-house.      Gold-adorned shone
tapestries upon the walls,      many wondrous sights
for each of the men,      who those who gaze on such things.
The bright building      was badly broken,
all the interior,      fast with iron-bands,
off hinges sprung asunder.      The roof alone survived
of all unhurt,      because the monster,      1000
besmeared with evil-deeds,      turned in flight,
despairing of life.      Not so easy is it
to flee--      do it he who will--
but of soul-bearers      of the sons of men,
of earth-dwellers,      one must seek,
compelled by fate,      that place readily
where his body-covering      in the bed of death sleeps
fast after the feast.      Then was the time and occasion
that the son of Healfdane      went to the hall;
the king himself wished      to partake of the feast.
Nor have I heard since      of a greater troop of kinsmen

around their treasure-giver      who bore themselves better.
They bowed to the benches,      fame-owning ones,
rejoiced in the feast,      accepted with ease[6]
many mead-cups      from their kinsmen,
the strong-minded ones,      in the hall of the high ones,
Hrothgar and Hrothulf.      Heorot inside was
filled with friends--      nothing of treachery
did the people of the Scyldings      perform then.
      The "Sword-of-Healfdane"      then gave to Beowulf      1020
a golden standard,      reward of victory,
adorned war-banner,      a helmet and a byrnie;
many saw      before the man brought it
a famous treasure-sword.      Beowulf drank
a cup on the hall-floor;      he needed to feel no shame
in the presence of the warriors      for the treasure-gift.
Nor have I heard      of four treasures,
gold-adorned, given      to others in a friendlier fashion
by many men      on the mead-bench.
Around the helm's roof,      upon the head-barrow,
it was bound with wire      to guard against slaughter,
so that file-leavings      might not severely
injure a storm-hardened one,      when a shield-warrior
must go      against hostile ones.
The protector of men then ordered      eight mares
with gold-plated bridles      led onto the hall-floor
inside the courtyards;      one of them stood
in a saddle shining with armor      ennobled with jewels.
That was the battle-seat      of the high-king,
when Healfdane's son      would perform      1040
in the sword-play.      Never at the battle-front lay down
the widely known warrior      when corpses fell.

---

[6]I have sometimes tried to keep the Germanic syntax, though it occasionally
seems awkward to modern readers, to give a sense of how the poem's phrasing
actually proceeds.

And then to Beowulf      over both of the two,
horses and weapons,      the protector of the Ingwins
gave power,      commanded him to use them well.
So manfully      the famous lord,
hoard-guardian of heroes,      for the unrush of battle gave
mares and heirlooms      such as one would never reproach,
one who wants to speak      truth according to what is right.
Yet then to each one      on the mead-bench
of those who with Beowulf      took the sea-voyage
the lord of men      gave treasures,
inherited relics,      and for the one commanded
gold repaid,      that one whom Grendel before
killed in wickedness,      as he would have more of them
had not wise god,      fate, and the man's courage
hindered it.      The measurer ruled all
of the race of men,      as he now still does.
Therefore understanding      is best everywhere,
the spirit's fore-thought.      He who long here                    1060
enjoys the world      in these days of strife
must experience much      of loved ones and enemies.
            There was song and sound      both together
before Healfdane's      battle-leader,
the pleasure-harp greeted      and tales often told
when in hall-games      Hrothgar's scop
along the mead-benches      would declaim:
with Finn's sons,      when that disaster befell them,
the hero of the half-Danes,      Hnaef of the Scyldings,
had to fall      in the Frisian slaughter.
Truly, not at all did Hildeburh      need to praise
the good faith of the Frisians;      guiltlessly was she
deprived of loved-ones,      sons and brothers,
by the shield-play--      they at birth doomed to fall
wounded by the spear.      That was a sad lady.
Not at all without reason      Hoc's daughter
mourned fate's-decree      after the morning came
when under the skies she      could see

the murder of kinsmen      where before she most held
joy in the world.      Battle took away all                    1080
of Finn's thanes      except only a few,
so that he could not      battle Hengest,
the prince's thane,                in the meeting-place,[7]
fight by any means,      nor crush in war
the miserable survivors.      But they offered them terms
so they fully cleared      for the Danes a second space
with a hall and throne,      so they could have
half control      with the sons of their enemies,
and the son of Folcwalda      each day
should honor the Danes      with treasure-gifts;
Hengest's troop      should honor with rings
even as much      with treasure-wealth,
plates of gold,      since he in the beer-hall
wished to build relations      with the Frisian folk.
Then they pledged      on the two sides
a firm compact of peace.      Finn to Hengest
declared oaths      with eager accord
that he held in honor,      by the counsel of wise men,
the suffering survivors,      and that no man,
neither in words nor deeds,      should break the treaty      1100
nor in cunning malice      ever complain of it,
though they found themselves following,      lordless,
the bane of their ring-giver,      when need made it so.
If any of the Frisians      audaciously spoke
of the murderous-hatred,      were reminded of it,
then the sword's edge      must come afterward.
      ⸙ The oath was carried out      and splendid gold
heaved up from the hoard.      The best of battle-warriors
of the soldier-Scyldings      was prepared for the fire.
In the fire it was      easy to see

---

[7]The metaphor *meeting-place* means battle or place of battle, but I have tried
in most instancies to keep the poet's figures of speech.

blood-stained byrnies,      a boar-image wrought in gold,
iron-hard boar-crest,      and many a nobleman
ruined by wounds,      notables slain in the slaughter.
Hildeburh then commanded      into the flames committed
her own son,      in Hnaef's fire,
the bone-vessel burnt,      placed in the fire.
On the uncle's shoulder      the woman grieved,
lamented with songs.      The warriors rose up;
the greatest of slaughter-fires      curled to the skies,
roared before the barrow--      heads melted,                1120
open wounds burst,      then blood sprung forth,
the body's hate-bites.      Flame swallowed all,
the greediest spirit,      of those whom battle took
from both peoples.      Their glory was gone.
        The warriors themselves then went      to go home,
deprived of friends,      to see Frisia,
home and citadel.      Hengest yet then
dwelt with Finn      in slaughter-stained winter
in utter misfortune;      he remembered his home,
although he could not      drive on the ocean
the ring-prowed ship.      The sea surged with storm,
strove against the wind;      winter-waves shut,
ice-binding,      till another year came
among the courtyards,      as now it still does,
that which always      observes its season,
glory-bright weather.      Then was winter departed,
the earth's bosom fair.      Anxious was the exile,
stranger to the courtyards;      he thought more surely
of vengeance      than of a sea-voyage,
if he could bring about      a bitter-moot,[8]                1140
because inside he remembered      the sons of the Jutes.
Thus he did not refuse      the world-custom
when Hunlafing      placed in his lap

---

[8]That is, a battle.

the battle-flame,      best of swords--
the edges of this sword were known      among the giants.
Likewise brave-in-spirit      Finn in turn got
a cruel sword-death      at his own home
when following the fierce fight      Guthlaf and Oslaf,
after their sea-journey,      complained of grief,
blamed them for a great deal of woe--      the restless spirit
couldn't remain in the breast.      Then was the hall reddened
with the blood of enemies;      also Finn was slain,
the king among his company,      and the queen taken.
The bowmen of the Scyldings      carried to their ship
all the house-possessions      of the king of the land
that they could find      at Finn's home,
jewels, cunningly cut gems.      On the sea-voyage
they brought to the Danes      the lordly lady,
led her to her people.      The song was sung,
tale of the singing-man.      Joy arose again,                    1160
bench-noise rang out.      Cupbearers proffered
wine from wondrous vessels.      Then Wealhtheow came forth,
went wearing gold rings      where the two good ones sat,
uncle and nephew;      their friendship was yet together,
each true to the other.      Likewise Hunferth the sage sat
at the feet of the Scylding's lord;      each trusted in his mind
that he had a great heart,      though with his kinsmen he was
never gracious at sword-play.      The Scylding lady then spoke:
"Take this cup,      my noble-lord,
giver of treasure.      Be joyful,
gold-friend of men,      and speak to the Geats
in gentle words,      as a man should do.
Be gracious with the Geats,      mindful of the gifts
you now have      from far and near.
Someone said to me      that you yourself wished to have
this warrior for a son.      Heorot is cleansed,
bright ring-hall;      enjoy while you can
the meed of the many,      and leave to your kin
folk and kingdom      when you must go forth

to see the creator.      I know of my                              1180
noble Hrothulf      that he will rule with honor
over the young warriors,      if you, friend of the Scyldings,
depart the world      sooner than he.
I expect that with good      he will pay
our sons,      if he bear in mind
what we did for his benefit,      for his desire
and his honor      in their youth."
She turned round the bench      where her sons,
Hrethric and Hrothmund,      and the sons of the soldiers,
the youth were all together.      There the good one sat,
Beowulf of the Geats,      between the two brothers.
A cup was brought to him      and friendly invitation
offered in words,      and wound gold
presented in gifts:      two arm-bands,
byrnie and rings,      and the largest torque
of those on earth      I have heard of.
Of the treasures of heroes      I have heard
of none better under heaven      since Hama carried away
to the bright citadel      the necklace of the Brosings,
the jewel and precious setting.      He fled the treachery      1200
of Eormenric,      gained long-lasting good.
Hygelac of the Geats,      had that circlet,
nephew of Swerting,      close by him later
when under the standard      he defended the treasure,
protected the battle-spoil.      Fate took him
after he sought out trouble      for pride,
feud with the Frisians.      He wore the treasure,
precious stones,      over the brimming sea,[9]
noble lord--      he fell under the shield.
The king's life      passed in to the power of the Franks,
breast-mail      and the necklace together;

---

[9]The original is more homey but difficult to translate, "the cupfull of waves."

worse warriors      rifled the slain
after the battle-slaughter.      The Geats got
the place-of-corpses.      The hall was seized with music.
          Wealhtheow spoke;      she said before the company:
"Enjoy this circlet,      beloved Beowulf,
young man, with health,      and use this corselet well,
treasure of the people,      and prosper truly.
Prove yourself with skill,      and to these boys be
kind in giving instruction.      I will requite you for that.  1220
You have brought it about      that far and near
all men      will praise you forever,
even as widely      as the sea surrounds
the walls of the home of the wind.      Be, while you live,
noble one, happy.      I properly grant you
the wealth of treasure.      Be to my sons
gracious in deeds,      protective of happiness.
Here each man is      true to the others,
mild of heart,      loyal to the lord of men.
The thanes are united,      the nation quite ready;
having drunk, the retainers      will do as I bid."
          She went to her seat.      There was the best of feasts.
The men drank wine--      they did not know fate,
dark decree of old,      as it was to happen
to many a man      after evening came--
and from them Hrothgar departed      to his dwelling,
king to his rest.      A countless number of men
guarded the hall,      as they often had done.
The bench-planks cleared,      it was overspread
with beds and cushions.      One of the beer drinkers,          1240
fearless and fated,      sunk to a hall-couch.
They set by their heads      battle-bosses,
bright shield-wood.      There on the bench
above the noble one      was easily to be seen
a battle-tall helmet,      a ringed byrnie,
a mighty spear.      It was their custom
that they often were ready,      with respect to fighting,

both at home and harrying,      and for either of them,
even in such times      as the need occurred
to their lord,      that folk was good.
              They sank to sleep.      A certain one sorely paid
for that evening-rest,      as had often happened to them
since Grendel guarded      the gold-hall,
committed crimes      until the end came,
death after sins.      That was seen,
known far and wide to men,      that an avenger still lived
after the hostile one,      for a long time
after the battle-care.      Grendel's mother,
lady, monster-woman,      remembered misery,
she who must dwell      in the terrible waters,              1260
cold currents,      since Cain was
sword-slayer      of his own brother,
father's kinsman;      Cain then departed blood-stained,
marked with murder,      fled the joys of men,
dwelt in the wastes.      Thence woke a multitude
of fated spirits;      of those Grendel was one,
hate-accursed foe      who at Heorot found
a waking man      awaiting battle.
There the monster      was at close grips with him;
but he was mindful      of the strength of his might,
the glorious gift      that god gave him
and for honor      left himself to the all-guardian
for comfort and support.      By them he overcame the fiend,
subdued the hell-spirit.      Then he left the high hall,
deprived of joy      to see the place of death,
enemy of mankind.      And his mother then yet,
greedy and gallow-minded,      wished to go
on a sorrowful venture,      to avenge her son's death.
              She came then to Heorot,      where the ring-Danes
slept throughout the hall.      Then there was soon              1280
reversal of fortune      for the men when
Grendel's mother entered.      The terror was less
even as much      as is a maid's skill,

that of a warrior-woman,      to weaponed-man's
when the decorated sword      forged with the hammer,
the blood-stained blade      with strong edges,
shears through      the boar upon the helmet opposite.
Then in the hall      was the hard-blade drawn,
swords over benches,      and many broad-shields
raised, firm in hands.      One forgot his helmet
and broad byrnie      when the horror seized him.
She was in haste,      wished to go thence
to save her life      when she was discovered.
Quickly she had      firmly grasped
one of the nobles,      then she went to the fen.
To Hrothgar he was      the dearest of the heroes
of the rank of retainer      of noble shield-warriors
between the two seas,      he whom she killed in bed,
a fame-rich man.      Nor was Beowulf there,
but in another building      assigned before,                1300
after the treasure-giving      to the famous Geat.
            A cry arose in Heorot.      Under the bloody one she
took the well-known hand.      Sorrow was renewed,
arose in the dwelling.      Nor was that exchange good,
which they must pay      on both parts
with the lives of friends.      Then was the old king,
gray battle-warrior,      troubled in heart
when he learned      the senior-thane
to be dead, the dearest one      no longer living.
Quickly was Beowulf      fetched to the chamber,
victory-blessed warrior.      Together before daybreak
went a certain one of the men,      noble champion,
himself with his companions      where the wise one awaited
whether for him the all-ruler      after the woeful tidings
ever wished to bring about      a change for the better.
The war-honorable one      then went along the floor with
his hand-picked retainers;      the hall-wood resounded
until he addressed      the leader in words,
lord of the Ingwins,      asked if it had been,

in view of the needful-summons,     an agreeable night.
          Hrothgar spoke,     protector of Scyldings:                    1320
"Ask not about joys;     sorrow is renewed
for the nation of the Danes.     Aeschere is dead,
Yrmenlaf's     elder brother,
my rune-counselor     and my advisor,
shoulder-companion     when in battle we
guarded our heads     when infantry clashed,
struck boar-figures.     So must a man be
noble, pre-eminent,     as Aeschere was.
A murderous-spirit, restless,     became in Heorot
his hand-slayer;     I do not know whither
it took its return,     rejoicing in its terrible food,
renowned for death.     She avenged the feud
in which yesterday night     you killed Grendel
by means of violence     in your firm clasp,
because too long     he lessened and destroyed
my people.     He fell in battle,
guilty of old,     and now the other has come far,
mighty evil-enemy,     wished to avenge her kin,
and has in feud     taken vengeance,                              1340
as it may appear to you,     to many a thane,
he who weeps in his heart     for the treasure-giver,
for his hard grief of mind.     Now the hand fails,
that which wrought     each one of your wishes.
Among the land-dwellers,     my people,
the hall-counselors,     I have heard said
that they saw     two such
great march-walkers,     alien spirits,
guard the moors.     One of them was,
such as they most certainly     could learn,
in the likeness of a woman;     the other misshapen one
trod the paths of exile     in a man's form,
except he was larger     than any other man.
That one in the old days     was named Grendel
by earth-dwellers;     nor did they know the father,

whether by him any other        secret spirits
were begat before.        They keep a hidden land,
wolf-slopes,        windy headlands,
dangerous fen-paths,        where a mountain-stream
under darkness of headlands        departs farther down,
a flood under the earth.        Nor is it far hence          1361
in mile-marks        that the mere stands.
Over it hang        frost-covered woods;
trees with firm roots        overshadow the water.
There each night may        one see a horrifying marvel:
fire on the flood.        None of the old ones lives
of the sons of men        who knows the bottom.
Morever the heath-stepper        harassed by hounds,
the strong hart with horns,        will seek the forest
put to flight from afar,        will first give up
his life on the shore,        before he will go in
to hide his head.        That is not a pleasant place.
Thence wave-turmoil        leaps up,
strives against the sky        when the wind stirs up
grievous storms        until the air darkens
and the heavens weep.        Now our help depends
again on you alone.        That land you do not yet know,
a dangerous place        where you might find
the much-sinning creature--        seek her if you dare.
For the feud I will        repay you wealth,                 1380
with ancient treasures,        as I did previously,
with wound gold,        if you come away from there."
        Beowulf spoke,        son of Ecgtheow:
"Do not grieve, wise one;        it is better for everyone
that he avenge his friend        than that he mourn greatly.
Each of us must        experience the end
of life in the world--        win glory before death
he who can.        That is best
afterwards for the warrior        no longer living.
Arise, guardian of the kingdom,        and go out quickly
to examine the track        of Grendel's kin.

I promise it to you:      he will not escape to protection,
neither in the bosom of the earth      nor into mountain wood
nor to the bottom of the sea,      go where he will.
Have patience      this day
with each of your woes      as I expect you will."
          The ancient one leaped up,      gave thanks to god,
to the mighty lord      for what the man spoke.
Then Hrothgar's horse      was saddled and bridled,
the horse with the braided mane;      the wise king                1400
rode well-equipped.      A troop of footmen marched,
shield-bearers.      Tracks were seen to go
far and wide      over the ground
along the forest paths      directly in front
over the mirky moor--      she bore
lifeless      the best of the young thanes
of those who together with Hrothgar      guarded the home.
The children of princes      traversed then
the steep rocky-slope,      climbed the narrows,
thin lonely-paths,      unknown courses,
precipitous cliffs,      houses of many water-demons.
He with a certain few      of the wise men
rode before      to examine the place,
until suddenly found      mountain trees
to lean over      grey stone,
a joyless wood.      Water stood underneath,
bloody and troubled.      To all of the Danes,
friends of the Scyldings,      for all the thanes
it was an affliction of the heart      to endure,
distress to each of the men,      when they came upon                1420
Aeschere's head      on the lake-cliff.
          The flood welled with blood--      people saw it so--
hot with blood.      A horn rang out betimes,
ready battle-song.      The foot troop all sat down.
They saw then along the water      many serpents,
strange sea-dragons      searching the lake,
as on headland-slopes      water-demons lie,

which in morning-time      often cause
a sorrowful journey      on the sail-road,
worms and wild-beasts.      They rushed away,
bitter and angry:      they heard the clear note,
the war-horn singing.      One of them a man of the Geats
deprived of life,      of wave-strife
with an arrow-bow,      so that a hard war-arrow
stuck in his vitals.      He was swimming the slower
in the waves      since death took him.
The strange wave-traveler      quickly in the wash was
sorely pressed,      attacked violently
with boar-spears,      savagely-hooked ones,
and drawn onto the headland.      The men inspected            1440
that ghastly guest.      Beowulf prepared himself
in war-garments;      not at all did he feel anxiety.
The battle-mail,      woven by hands,
broad and cunningly adorned,      must test the lake--
it knew how to protect      the bone-chamber
so that the battle-grip,      wrathful malice-grasp,
could not injure      his heart, his vitals,
and the shining helmet      guarded his head,
he who must stir up      the mere-bottom
to seek the surging water,      ennobled with treasure,
encircled with lordly-chains,      as in days of yore
a weapons-smith had fashioned it,      wrought with wonders,
set with boar-figures,      so that afterwards neither
sword nor-battle-mace      could bite into it.
Then not the smallest      of strength-aids,
which Hrothgar's spokesman      lent him in need,
was the long-hilted sword      named Hrunting.
It was alone foremost      of inherited-treasures;
the edge was iron,      adorned with poison-plants,
hardened in battle-blood.      It had never failed in a fight   1460
any one of the men      who enclosed it in his hands,
he who dared to pursue      perilous exploits to the
dwelling-place of enemies.      That was not the first quest

in which it must perform     an act of courage.
Truly Ecglaf's kin     did not think
of mighty toils,     what he said before,
drunk with wine,     when he lent that weapon
to a better warrior.     He did not dare
to risk life     under the turmoil of waves
to perform an act of courage--     there he lost glory,
valor-fame.     The other one was not so,
since he had     prepared himself for war.
          Beowulf spoke,     Ecgtheow's son:
"It seems now, renowned     son of Healfdane,
wise king,     that I am eager for a journey,
gold-friend of men,     what we two spoke of before.
If at your need     I should
be deprived of life,     that you should always be to me,
departed away,     in the place of a father:
be a protector     to my kinsmen-thanes,                    1480
close-comrades,     if battle takes me.
Likewise, the treasures     you have given to me,
beloved Hrothgar,     send to Hygelac.
The lord of the Geats,     son of Hrethel,
will understand by the gold     when he sees that treasure
that I found a good one     with manly virtues,
a ring-giver,     and I enjoyed it while I could.
And allot Hunferth     the ancestral relic,
glorious patterned-sword,     the widely-known man
to have the hard-edge.     With Hrunting I for myself
will achieve glory,     or death will take me."
          After those words     the man of the weather-Geats
hastened eagerly--     not at all did he wish
to await an answer.     The surging lake received
the battle-warrior.     Then it was a time
before he could     descry the bottom.
Soon she found out,     who fiercely ravenous guarded
the expanse of the flood     for a hundred half-years,
grim and greedy,     that there a certain man

explored from above       that home of alien-creatures.        1500
She grasped then towards him,       siezed the battle-warrior
in horrible grips,        none the sooner injured
the healthy body;        the rings outside protected him,
so that she could not puncture       with hostile fingers
the war-covering,        interlocked mail-coat.
When she came to the bottom       the sea-wolf
then bore the prince of rings       to her dwelling
so that he could not,       no matter how brave he was,
wield weapons,        but many of the monsters
in the lake harassed him,       many sea-beasts
with warlike tusks       broke the war-shirt,
pursued the giant one.       Then the man perceived
that he was in an enemy hall,       he knew not what sort,
where none of the water       in any way harmed him,
nor could it touch him,       sudden rush of the flood,
because of a roofed-hall.       He saw fire-lights,
gleaming flames       shining brightly.
         The good man then spotted       the earth-cursed one,
mighty mere-woman.       A mighty rush he gave
with his sword,       did not withhold hand-swing              1520
so that on her head       the ring-adorned blade rang out
a greedy war-song.       Then the guest found
that the battle-light       would not bite,
injure the vitals,       but the edge failed
the nobleman at need.       It had before endured many
hand-to-hand battles,       often cut through helmets,
war-garments of the death-fated;       that was the first time
for the fierce heirloom       that its glory failed.
Again was he resolute,       remembering glory,
not slow in courage,       kinsman of Hygelac.
The wrathful warrior       then discarded the patterned-sword
bound with serpent-figures       so it lay on the ground,
strong and steel-edged.       He trusted in the strength
of his mighty hand-grip--       so must a man do
when in battle he       thinks to win

enduring fame,      cares not at all about life.
The man of the war-Geats      then seized by the shoulder
Grendel's mother--      he did not mourn for that feud.
The strong one flung into the fight      the mortal foe
when he was enraged,      so that she fell on the hall-floor.  1540
She quickly after      paid him requital
with fierce grips      and seized him against her.
The strongest of men      then stumbled disheartened
so that he fell,      foot-warrior.
She then sat on her hall-guest      and drew her knife,
broad and bright-edged;      she wished to avenge her son,
her only progeny.      On his shoulder lay
the woven breast-net:      that saved his life--
it withstood entry      against point and edge.
Then Ecgtheow's son      had perished
under the earth,      champion of the Geats,
but the battle-byrnie      provided help,
hard war-net,      and holy god
brought him battle-victory--      the wise lord,
ruler of the heavens,      decided it rightly,
quite easily,      once he again stood up.
He saw then among the armor      a victory-blessed blade,
an old monstrous sword      with firm edges,
honor-memorial of men;      that was the best of weapons,
though it was larger      than any other man                1560
could carry      into battle-play,
good and noble,      the work of giants.
He grasped the ring-hilt,      adventurer of the Scyldings,
fierce and battle-grim,      drew the ring-decorated one,
despairing of life,      and angrily struck
so that it grievously gripped      against her neck.
Bone-rings broke;      the blade passed entirely through
the death-fated flesh-home.      She crashed on the floor.
The sword was bloody;      the soldier rejoiced in the deed.
        The spark gleamed;      a light issued within,
even as from heaven      the candle of the sky

shines brightly.      He afterwards gazed at the hall,
went along the wall,        raised the weapon,
hard in its hilts,        Hygelac's thane,
wrathful and resolute.        Nor was the blade worthless
to the battle-warrior,        but he quickly wished
to repay Grendel        for the many war-rushes
that he wrought        on the west-Danes,
much more often        than on one venture,
when he        slew while dreaming                                 1580
Hrothgar's hearth-companions,        devoured sleeping ones,
fifteen men        of the people of the Danes
and carried off        a second fifteen likewise,
loathsome booty.        He gave him requital for that,
fierce champion,        when he saw Grendel lying
battle-weary        in his resting place,
lifeless,        as he had previously harmed him
in battle at Heorot.        The corpse sprung wide open
when after death        it suffered a blow,
stern sword-stroke,        and the head was hewed off.
        Soon the wise        men saw,
those who with Hrothgar        gazed on the water,
that the wave-turmoil was        all mingled,
the lake stained with blood.        The gray-haired
old ones spoke together        concerning the good man
that they did not expect        that nobleman again,
triumphing in victory,        to come seeking
the famous king.        Then it seemed certain to many
that the she-wolf        had slain him.
Then came the ninth hour of the day;        the brave Scyldings  1600
abandoned the headlands.        The gold-friend of men
departed thence home.        The guests sat
sick at heart        and stared at the mere.
They wished but did not expect        that they would see him,
their friend-lord.        Then that sword began,
from the battle-blood,        the war-blade to dissolve
into battle-icicles;        that was a certain wonder

that it all melted      most like ice
when the father loosens      the bond of frost,
unwinds winter-fetters,      who has the power
over season and time:      that is the true god.
Nor took he from that place,      man of the weather-Geats,
more precious possessions,      though he saw many there,
than the head      and the hilt together,
adorned treasure;      the sword had melted before,
the wave-patterned blade burnt up.      Too hot was the blood
of the poisonous alien-spirit      who died therein.
      Soon was he swimming;      he who had known in struggle
the fall of the enemy      quickly swam up through the water.
The surging waves were      all cleansed,                    1620
a vast area,      since the alien-spirit
relinquished life-days      and this transitory world.
The protector of seafarers      then came to land,
swimming stout-hearted,      rejoiced in sea-plunder,
in the might-burden      of that which he had with him.
They went to him together,      gave thanks to god;
the trusty troop of thanes      rejoiced for their leader
because they were able      to see him sound.
Then from the strong one      helmet and byrnie
were quickly loosened.      The lake grew still,
water under the clouds,      stained with slaughter-blood.
They went forth thence      on the walking-tracks
glad in spirit      and met the road,
the known ways.      The king-bold men
bore the head      from the lake-cliff
with difficulty,      each pair
of the brave ones.      Four had to
tote with toil      Grendel's head
on the battle-pole      to the gold-hall,
until presently      the war-keen                    1640
fourteen      of the Geats came
walking with courage.      The lord of men,
brave one with his troop      trod the mead-place.

Then came in walking      the senior of the thanes,
the deed-keen one      honored with fame,
the hale battle-bold one      to greet Hrothgar.
Then onto the floor      Grendel's head
was brought by the hair      terrible before men,
where the men had drunk      and the lady with them:
the men saw      a wondrous spectacle.
      Beowulf spoke,      son of Ecgtheow:
"Hear me, son of Healfdane:      we have happily brought you,
prince of the Scyldings,      this sea-plunder,
the token of glory      on which you look here.
Not that easily      I endured with my life
in battle under the water,      dared that deed
with difficulty.      Immediately had
that battle ended,      except god shielded me.
Nor in battle could I      achieve anything
with Hrunting,      though that weapon be able.                          1660
But the ruler of men      granted to me
that I saw hanging      on the wall a beautiful,
huge old-sword--      most often he guides
the one lacking friends--      so that I drew the weapon.
In the struggle I slew,      when the chance was granted me,
the guardian of the hall.      Then that battle-sword
burnt up, wave-patterned one,      as that blood sprung out,
hottest of battle-gore.      I carried that hilt
thence from the fiends,      vengeance for evil-deeds,
death-slaughter of the Danes,      as it was fitting.
I promised you then      that in Heorot you could
sleep free from trouble      with the men of your troop
and each of the thanes,      your beloved ones,
veterans and young warriors,      so you need not fear him,
lord of the Scyldings,      on his behalf,
mortal-injury to men,      as you did before."
      Then was the golden hilt      given into the hand
of the old warrior,      to the gray battle-leader,
the ancient giant-work.      After the fall of those devils

it passed into the possession      of the lord of the Danes,    1680
work of wondrous smiths;      and when the angry one,
god's enemy,      gave up this world,
guilty of murder,      and his mother also,
it passed into the power      of the best
of earthly kings      between the two seas,
of those who dealt out treasures      in the Danish region.
          Hrothgar spoke,      examined the hilt,
old remnant;      on it was written the beginning
of ancient strife,      since the Flood slew,
sea poured upon      the race of giants.
They fared ill--      that was a people estranged
from the eternal lord.      The ruler gave them
a last reward      through the surging of the water.
Likewise on the hilt      of bright gold
it was rightly marked      in runes,
established and said      for whom that sword,
best of iron ones,      spiral-hilted and serpent-decorated,
was first made.      Then the wise one spoke,
son of Healfdane--      all were silent:
"That indeed one may say,      he who does truly and rightly    1700
by the people      and remembers all far back,
old guardian of the homeland,      that this man was
born the better one.      Your fame is borne up
throughout the wide-regions,      my friend Beowulf,
yours over each of the nations.      Guard it all patiently,
strength with prudence of mind.      With you I shall keep my
friendship, as we two first spoke.      You must be a comfort
altogether long-lasting      to your people
with good fortune to help you.      Heremod was not so
to the sons of Ecgwela,      the honor-Scyldings,
nor did he grow as they desired,      but to murder
and death-slaughter      for the people of the Danes.
The swollen-hearted one killed      board-companions,
shoulder-comrades,      until he turned alone,
famous lord,      from the joys of men,

though glorious god      with the pleasures of power
exalted him among mighty ones,      advanced him forward
over all men;      however in him the spirit grew,
a breast-hord eager for blood.      He did not give rings
to the Danes by choice.      Joyless he remained,              1720
so that he suffered      the toil of hardship,
enduring affliction.      Instruct yourself by that:
understand manly virtue.      Wise in winters, I tell
this tale in comparison with you.      It is wonderful to say
how mighty god      with spacious spirit
gives wisdom      to the race of men,
land and nobility.      He wields power over all.
Sometimes he permits      a man's heart-thoughts
to turn to his beloved home,      one of glorious kin,
gives him in his homeland      to hold
the joys of earth,      a stronghold of men,
places in him such power      over portions of the world,
broad kingdoms,      that because of lack of wisdom
he himself cannot      conceive his end.
He lives in abundance;      no creature hinders him,
illness nor old age,      nor does malice-grief
darken his heart,      nor does enmity anywhere,
sword-hate, show itself,      but the world turns
entirely to his pleasure.      He does not know that evil
until within him      a great deal of pride[10]              1740
grows and flourishes      when the guardian sleeps,
keeper of the soul.      That sleep is too firmly
bound with business,      the slayer very near,
he who with the arrow-bow      shoots wickedly.
Then it is in the mind,      struck under the helmet by
a bitter arrow--      he does not know how to guard himself--
the perverse, weird promptings      of the cursed spirit.
It seems to him too little      that he ruled so long.

---

[10]The Old English word is *ofer-hygd*, literally, excess of mind or heart.

Avaricious, hostile-hearted,      he does not honorably give
gold-plated treasures,      and he disregards
and forgets the future,      because before god gave him,
heaven's ruler,      a portion of honor.
In the end it      comes to pass afterwards
that the body-covering,      transitory, decays,
the doomed one falls;      another grasps, too,
he who without regret      deals out heirlooms,
ancient treasures of men,      heeds not terrors.
Guard against that grievous-ill,      beloved Beowulf,
best of men,      and choose the better,
eternal benefits.      Do not heed pride,                    1760
great champion;      the glory of your might is now
only for a while.      It is soon afterwards
that sickness or sword      will strip your strength,
or the fire's grasp      or the flood's surging
or the mace's grip      or the spear's flight
or horrible old age,      or the brightness of your eyes
will become feeble and darken.      Presently it will be
that death will overpower      you, warrior.
So I ruled the ring-Danes      a hundred half-years
under the skies      and saved them in war
against many tribes      throughout this middle-earth,
from spears and swords,      so that I do not deem
anyone an adversary      under the expanse of heaven.
Hear me: a change came      in this my homeland,
affliction after joy,      once Grendel became,
the ancient adversary,      my invader.
I continually bore      that persecution,
great heart-care.      So thanks be to god,
the eternal lord,      that I remained alive,
so that after old hardship      I may stare                    1780
with my eyes      on that sword-bloody head.
Go now to your seat;      conduct the feast-joy,
war-worthy one.      Between us two must be a great many
shared treasures      when it is morning."

         The Geat was joyful in heart,        went at once to
seek his seat        as the wise one commanded.
Then again as before        a feast was graciously made ready
for the valor-famous ones,        hall-sitters,
anew.  The helm of night        blackened,
dark over the troop-men.        The veterans all arose.
The gray-haired one wished        to seek his bed,
the ancient Scylding.        The Geat, famous
shield-warrior,        desired immeasurably to rest.
Soon a hall-thane        led him forth
weary from the adventure        in distant regions,
one who for courtesy        observed all
of the thane's needs        such as in those days
battle-travelers        used to have.
• The great-hearted one rested himself;        the hall rose up
spacious and gold-adorned.        The guest slept inside        1800
until the shining raven,        the blithe-heart announced
the joy of heaven.        Then came the bright one hurrying,
light after shadow.        The warriors hastened;
the nobles were        again eager to go
to their people;        they wished,
bold-spirited visitors,        to seek their ship far thence.
The brave one then asked        that Hrunting be borne
to the son of Ecglaf,        asked him to take his sword,
precious iron-one.        He thanked him for the loan,
said he considered        the battle-friend good,
mighty in war,        not at all blamed in words
the sword's edge.        That was a noble man.
         Then the warriors were        venture-ready,
eager in armor.        Then went the prince to the dais,
the worthy one among the Danes        to where the other was.
The hale battle-bold one        greeted Hrothgar.
Beowulf spoke,        son of Ecgtheow:
"Now we seafarers        wish to say that,
come from afar,        we are anxious
to seek Hygelac.        Here we were amply        1820

entertained with pleasures;      you treated us well.
If then on earth I      can achieve
any more      of your mind-love,
lord of men,      than I have done thus far
by war-works,      I am ready immediately.
If I hear      over the expanse of sea
that surrounding nations      threaten you with terror,
as enemies sometimes      have done,
I will bring you      a thousand thanes,
heroes to help you.      I know with respect to Hygelac,
lord of the Geats,      although he be young,
shepherd of the people,      that he will support me
in words and works      so that I may honor you well
and support you,      bear spear-shafts
with the help of strength,      where you are in need of men.
If then Hrethric,      lord's son, decides to come
to him to the house of the Geats,      he can find there
many friends.      Distant lands are
better sought      by one who himself is strong."

      Hrothgar spoke      in answer to him:                    1840
"The wise lord      sent that speech
into your mind;      nor have I heard a man
so young in life      make a speech more wisely.
You are strong in might      and wise in mind,
sound in speech.      I consider it a likelihood,
if it happens      that the spear,
battle most fierce,      takes the son of Hrethel,
your prince,      shepherd of the people,
disease or the sword,      and you have your life,
that the sea-Geats      would not have a better one
to choose,      any king,
hoard-guardian of heroes,      if you wished to rule
the kingdom of your kinsmen.      Your mind's-heart
continues to please me well,      beloved Beowulf.
You have brought it about      that between the folk,
peoples of the Geats      and the spear-Danes,

will be shared friendship,      and strife will rest,
malice-hatred       that they endured before.
There will be while I rule      the wide kingdom
shared treasures,      many others                          1860
to greet with goods      over the gannet's-bath.
The ring-necked one must      bring over the sea
gifts and tokens of love.      I know the nations will be,
both toward foe and toward friend,      made fast,
blameless in everything      in the old way."
Then inside the protector of men,      Healfdane's kinsman,
yet gave him      twelve treasures,
commanded him with those gifts      to seek in safety
his beloved people      and speedily to come again.
The nobly good king,      lord of the Scyldings,
then kissed      the best of thanes
and took him by the neck;      tears fell from him,
the gray-haired one.      It was the expectation of both,
the one very wise with age      and the second more so,
that he thereafter      would not see him,
brave in speech.      To him the man was too dear,
so that he could not restrain      the breast-surging,
but in heart, in mind bonds      firmly fixed him,
burned in the blood      in silent longing
after the dear one.      From him thence Beowulf,             1880
gold-proud battle-warrior,      trod the grassy ground,
triumphing in treasure.      The sea-goer awaited
the owning-lord,      that which rode at anchor.
Then in their going      was the gift of Hrothgar
often praised.      That was a peerless king,
blameless in everything,      until old age took him
from the joys of power,      that which oft injures many.
        The very brave ones      then came to the sea,
the troop of youths;      they bore ring-nets,
interlocked mail-shirts.      The coast-guard observed
the return-journey of the men,      as he had done before.
Not with insult      from the cliff's promontory

did he greet the guests,        but rode together with them,
said that the welcome ones        from the Weders' nation,
soldiers in bright armor,        might go to their ship.
There on the sand was        the sea-spacious ship,
laden with war-garments,        the ring-prowed one,
with mares and heirlooms.        The mast towered
over Hrothgar's        treasured possessions.
He gave a sword        bound in gold                                    1900
to the boat-guardian        so that afterwards he was
for that treasure the more honored        on the mead-bench,
that inherited-survivor.        He departed in the ship,
drove for deep water,        quit the land of the Danes.
Then from the mast was        a certain sea-garment,
a sail fixed with a hawser.        The sea-wood groaned:
the wind over the waves        did not hinder the journey
there for the wave-floater.        The sea-goer fared on,
the foamy-necked one floated        forward over the waves,
the bound-prowed one        over the sea-currents,
so they could spot        the cliffs of the Geats,
the known headlands.        The ship pressed upward,
pushed by the air,        and stood on land.
The eager harbor-guard        was quickly at the water,
who for a long time before        gazed afar,
at the current anxious        for the beloved men.
He moored to the beach        the broad-breasted ship,
fixed it with anchor-ropes,        that the force of the waves
might the less drive it away,        winsome-wooded one.
The nobles' treasure        was then commanded borne up,        1920
armor and plated-gold.        Nor was it far for them
thence to seek        the giver of treasures,
Hygelac, Hrethel's son,        where he dwelt at home,
himself with companions        near the sea-wall.
        The building was splendid,        the princely-famed king
high in his hall,        Hygd very young,
wise, well-settled,        though Haereth's daughter
had passed        few winters

within the fortress.        Nor was she poor so, though,
nor too niggardly with gifts        of precious-treasures
to the people of the Geats.        Modthrytho waged,[11]
froward folk's-queen,        fearful crimes.
No brave one        of her dearer companions
except a noble lord        dared to risk
that by day        he gaze upon her with his eyes,
lest he count on having        death-bonds, hand-woven,
commanded for himself.        Quickly thereupon
after the hand-grip        it was determined by the sword,
that the shadow-patterned one        must settle it,
make known the killing-evil.        It is not a queenly custom   1940
in a lady to do such a thing,        though she be beautiful,
for a peace-weaver        to wrest of life
a beloved man        after imagined-injury.
However, Hemming's kinsman        put a halt to that.
Ale-drinkers        said something more,
that she brought about fewer        great afflictions,
evil acts        after she was
given gold-adorned        to the young champion,
precious one to the nobles,        she sought the journey
on the brown sea        to Offa's hall-floor
according to her father's bidding.        There on the throne
she afterwards rightly        enjoyed living,
her fated life-span        famous for virtue,
held noble-love        for the prince of heroes,
of all mankind,        of what has been told to me,
the best between        the two seas
of an august race.        Therefore Offa was
with gifts and in battles,        widely honored,
a spear-keen man.        He ruled his homeland

---

[11]One of the themes of *Beowulf* is what makes a good king or a bad king,
good retainer or bad retainer, good queen or bad queen. Modthrytho, in
contrast to Wealhtheow and Hygd, is a bad queen.

with wisdom.       Thence Eomer was born,                      1960
a help to heroes,       Hemming's kinsman,
descendant of Garmund        crafty in conflict.
     ✤ The brave one left then       with his hand-troop,
along the beach        walked the sea-plain,
the wide shore.       The world-candle shone,
sun hastening to the south.       They completed the journey,
went with courage        inside the stronghold
to where the protector of men,       killer of Ongentheow,
the young war-king,       the good one we have heard
to share rings.       Hygelac was
speedily made aware        of Beowulf's exploit,
that there in the citadel        the protector of warriors
with shield-companions        had come alive,
unharmed from the battle-play,       and approached the court.
The interior hall       was quickly cleared
for the foot-soldiers       as the mighty one ordered.
He who survived the battle       then sat near him,
kinsman with kinsman,       after the liege-lord
had greeted the loyal one       with a formal speech,
with earnest words.       Throughout the hall-building        1980
among the mead-cups       moved Haereth's daughter,
beloved by the people,       bore the wine-bottle
to the hands of the Haenas.[12]       Hygelac began
courteously to question       his comrade
in the high hall.       His curiosity burst forth
concerning what the adventures were       of the sea-Geats:
"How did it befall you in your journey,       beloved Beowulf,
when you suddenly       resolved far away
to seek strife       over the salt water,
battle at Heorot?       Did you for Hrothgar

---

[12]The text appears to read *hœ num*, which is probably another name for some of the Geats.  Some scholars prefer the emended *Hœðnum*, which may also be a Nordic tribal name, but looks dangerously close to "heathens."

in any way better     the widely known woes
of the nation for the famous one?     In this heart's-care I
seethed with grief-surgings,     did not trust in the venture
of my beloved man.     I long asked
that you by no means approach     the murderous-spirit,
permit the south-Danes     themselves to settle
the war with Grendel.     I speak thanks to god
because I can     see you sound."
          Beowulf spoke,     son of Ecgtheow:
"That is not secret,     Lord Hygelac,                          2000
to many men,     the famous meeting
of Grendel's and mine,     what battle
was in that place     where he performed
a multitude of sorrows     against the victory-Scyldings,
miseries for ever.     I avenged all that,
so any of the kin     of Grendel over the earth
need not boast     of that daybreak-clash,
he who lives the longest     of that loathed race
encircled in wickedness.     I first came there
to the ring-hall     to greet Hrothgar;
soon the famous one,     son of Healfdane,
after he knew     my heart,
assigned me a seat     next to his own sons.
The troop was in delight,     nor saw I in the wide world
under heaven's vault     among hall-sitters
greater mead-joy.     Betimes the famous queen,
peace-pledge of peoples,     would pass throughout the hall,
encouraged her young son;     often to a soldier she gave
twisted rings     before she went to her seat.
Sometimes for the veterans,     for the men on the end,     2020
Hrothgar's daughter     bore ale-cups.
Then I heard     the hall-sitters
name her Freawaru,     when she gave to the heroes
the stud-adorned vessel.     She is promised,
young, gold-adorned,     to the noble son of Froda.
The friend of the Scyldings,     guardian of the kingdom,

has brought that about     and considers it good counsel
that with the woman     he set right the strife,
a portion of the deadly-feud.     Very seldom anywhere
after the fall of a prince     for a little while
does the death-spear lie down,     though the bride avail.
This then may displease     the lord of the Heathobards
and each of the thanes     of that people,
when with the woman     he walks on the hall-floor,
noble attendant of the Danes     nobly entertained.
On him shines     the relic of ancestors,
hard and ring-adorned,     treasure of the Heathobards,
while they could wield     those weapons,
until they led to disaster,     shield-play,
of beloved companions     and their own lives.          2040
          Then one says at beer,     he who sees the ringed one,
an old ash-warrior,     he who fully remembers
the spear-killing of men--     in him is a grim heart--
sad of spirit he begins     to tempt, through
the thoughts of his heart,     of his mind, a young champion,
to kindle war-evil,     and utters this speech:
'Can you, my friend,     recognize the sword
that your father     bore to the fight
under his war mask     the last time,
the precious iron one,     when the Danes slew him,
valiant Scyldings,     ruled the battlefield,
when Withergyld lay dead     after the fall of heroes?
Now here a son of the slayers,     I know not which,
triumphing in treasures,     walks on the hall-floor,
boasts of murder     and bears the heirloom
which you by right     should possess.'
He urges so and recalls     each of the occasions
in grievous words     until the time comes
that the woman's thane,     for the deeds of the father,
sleeps blood-stained     from the bite of the sword,          2060
having forfeited his life.     The other thence
escapes him, living,     and knows the land completely.

Then on both sides      the sworn oath of the men
is broken      after deadly-enmity
wells up in Ingeld,      and in him the love-of-woman
after grief-surgings      becomes cooler.
Concerning that, I do not find      the Heathobards' favor,
their part of the peace      with the Danes, honest,
in firm friendship.      I must speak on
still about Grendel      so that you will know fully,
giver-of-rings,      concerning what thereupon became
a hand-rush of heroes.      After heaven's gem
glided over the ground,      the ghost came angrily,
horrible evening-grim one      to seek us
where we, safe,      guarded the hall.
For Hondscio there was      a battle impending,
mortal disaster for the fated one;      he lay closest,
girded warrior.      Grendel became
the mouth-slayer      of the famed young thane,
the beloved man,      entirely swallowed the body.                2080
None the sooner then yet,      empty-handed,
the bloody-toothed killer,      mindful of destruction,
wished to go out      of the gold-hall,
but, famous for might,      he tested mine,
grasped with eager hand.      His glove hung,
huge and horrifying,      fast with cunning-bonds,
ingeniously      all arrayed
with devil's skills      and with dragon's skins.
Brave deed-maker,      he wished to put me,
unsinning,      inside there,
one of many.      It could not be so,
since in wrath I      stood upright.
It is too long to relate      how I repaid requital
the enemy of the people      for each of his evils.
There, my lord,      I honored
your people with actions.      He escaped away,
for a little while      enjoyed life-pleasures.
However, his right hand      remained as a sign

in Heorot, and he    went thence wretched,
mournful at heart,    fell to the mere-bottom.       2100
For that deadly fight    the friend of the Scyldings
greatly repaid me    with plated gold,
with many treasures,    after morning came
and we had    sat down to feast.
There was story and music,    the aged Scylding
having heard of many things    related from far back.
Sometimes the battle-bold one    with delight greeted
the harp, joy-wood,    sometimes told a tale,
true and sorrowful,    sometimes strange tidings
reckoned rightly,    large-hearted king.
The ancient war-man,    bound in old age,
sometimes began again    to speak to the young soldiers
of strength in battle.    Inside his heart welled up
when, wise in winters,    he remembered a wealth of things.
        So inside there    the whole day
we took pleasure    until another night
came upon men.    Then quickly afterwards
Grendel's mother was    eager for grief-vengeance;
she journeyed sorrowfully.    Death took her son,
Weathers' war-hatred.    The horrible woman       2120
avenged her son,    slew a man
valorously:    there for Aeschere was,
wise old counselor,    a departure from life.
Nor could they,    the people of the Danes,
when morning came,    burn him in fire,
death-weary one,    nor lay him on the pyre,
beloved man.    She carried out that body,
a fiend's embraces    under a mountain stream.
To Hrothgar that was    the bitterest of sorrows
of those that long beset    the leader of the people.
Then the king, fierce in mind,    entreated me
by your life    that in the tumult of waters I
do noble deeds,    risk life,
perform something glorious.    He promised me a reward.

Then in the flood,      as is widely known,
I found the grim, terrible      ground-guardian.
Between us two awhile there was      a hand-joining.[13]
The water welled with gore,      and with might-edges
I cut off the head      of Grendel's mother
in the war-hall.      Not easily thence                    2140
I bore away life:      then I was not yet fated to die.
But the protector of men      afterwards gave me
many treasures,      Healfdane's heir.
So the nation-king      lived according to customs:
In the rewards by no means      had I lost
might's meed,      but he gave me treasures,
the son of Healfdane,      according to my own judgment,
which I wish to bring      to you, warrior-king,
to bestow with honors.      Still it is entirely on you
that favors depend.      I have few
close kinsmen      except you, Hygelac."

        He commanded brought in      the boar's-head standard,
the battle-tall helmet,      the gray byrnie,
the adorned war-sword,      and afterwards delivered a speech:
"Hrothgar gave me      this battle-gear,
wise lord.      He commanded in particular terms
that I first tell you      its legacy.
King Heorogar,      he said, had it,
leader of the Scyldings,      for a long while;
none the sooner wished he      to give to his son,        2160
the noble Heoroweard,      though he were loyal to him,
the breast-covering.      Enjoy it all well!
I heard that with the accoutrements      four mares,
swift, identical,      followed behind,
apple-yellow ones--      on him he bestowed the honor
of horses and precious things.      So must a kinsman do,

---

[13]The Old English hand-gemæne means "hand-meeting" or "hand-sharing,"
a metaphor for hand-to-hand combat.

not weave for another      nets of malice
with secret cunning        to arrange the death
of a close companion.      To Hygelac, hard in affliction,
the nephew was       very loyal,
and to every one of the others      mindful of pleasures.
I heard that to Hygd      he gave the neck-ring,
decorated treasure-wonder,      that Wealhtheow gave him,
daughter of a king,      and three horses also,
graceful and saddle-bright;      afterwards her breast
was ennobled      by receiving that ring.
        So Ecgtheow's son      showed courage,
a man known for battles,      for good deed;
he acted according to decree,      by no means drinking slew
hearth-companions.      Nor was a fierce heart in him,      2180
but of the race of men      he was greatest in might--
the ample gift      that god gave him
guarded the battle-bold one.      He was long despised,
as the men of the Geats      did not account him good,
nor did the lord of the Weders      wish to do him
much honor      on the mead-bench.
They strongly suspected      that he were slack,[14]
an inactive nobleman.      A change came
to the glory-blessed one      for each of those griefs.
        The protector of men then commanded      fetched in,
battle-famed king,      Hrethel's remnant
adorned with gold,      nor was there then among the Geats
a better jeweled-treasure      in the form of a sword.
That he laid      on Beowulf's lap,
and gave him      seven thousand hides of land,
a dwelling and a lord's-throne.      To them both together
in that country      was the leadership hereditary,
land, inheritance,      for the other more so

---

[14]Beowulf was a *kolbitur*, that is, a male Cinderella who had an inauspicious childhood but grew into a hero.

in the wide kingdom      where he was nobler.
          After that passed,      in later days,                    2200
since in the crash of battle      Hygelac lay dead,
and battle-swords      under shield-coverings
became the slayers      of Heardred
when hard, fierce warriors,      the battle-Scylfings
sought him      among the victory-folk,
out of enmity attacked      the nephew of Hereric,
the broad kingdom      afterwards passed
into the hand of Beowulf.      He ruled well
for fifty winters,      was then an old king,
ancient homeland-guardian,      until one began
to rule, a dragon      in the dark nights,
he who in his high house      watched a hoard,
in a steep stone-barrow.      A path lay beneath,
unknown to men.      There into the inside he went,
I know not which man,      . . . seized[15]
from the heathen hord      in hand . . .
a shining treasure.      He [avenged] that afterwards,
although he, sleeping,      was deceived by trickery,
the thief's craft.      When the folk-burner
discovered that,      that he was enraged.                    2220
Not at all by strength      [did he enter] the worm-hoard
the power of his own wishes,      he who sorely injured,
but out of grievous-need,      a slave of I know not which
of the sons of heroes      who fled hate-blows
in need . . .      and there entered inside,
a sin-furtive man.      Soon was a time of envy.
By the visitant      the horror stood;

---

[15]While several pages of the manuscript exhibit lacunae, fuzziness, or even scorching, this section of folio 179 is terribly damaged. Some scholars believe it may have been intentionally erased. Translation in this section ranges from dangerous to impossible. Occasionally in such instances or when the syntax is unmanageably difficult I have added a word or two; such cases I designate with brackets.

however . . .
shape . . . .
Then disaster happened:      [he took]
a precious cup--    there were many such
ancient treasures    in the earth-house
just as in the old days     I know not which of men,
a prince of the people,    a pensive-minded one
hid there     a vast legacy
of precious treasures.              Death took all of them
in earlier times,     and the one then yet,
a veteran of the nation     who longest dwelt there,
a guardian mourning for his friends,    expected the same,
that he might enjoy    a little time                    2240
the long-kept treasures.     The barrow, quite ready,
stood on a plain     near the surf,
new beside the bluff,    secured with enclosing-craft.[16]
Inside there he bore,    guardian of rings,
a hoard-worthy portion    of the treasure of noblemen,
plated gold,    and spoke a few words:
        "Hold now, you earth,    now that heroes cannot,
the possessions of men;    indeed, it was bravely got
from you before.    War-death,
dire life-bale,    took each of the men
of my nation,    those who gave up this life,
saw hall-joys.    I have no one who might carry
the sword or polish    the plated cup,
dear drinking vessel.    The veterans have gone elsewhere.
The hard helmet,    adorned with gold,
must be deprived of its plates.    The polishers sleep,
those who should prepare    battle-grim gear.
And likewise the war-cloak:    in battle it lasted
over the shattering of shields    the bite of iron ones;

---

[16]The Old English *nearo-cræft*, probably means "skill in enclosing" or "ability to build enclosures."

it will crumble after the men.        Nor may the ringed byrnie  2260
along with its war-leader        travel widely
by the side of heroes.        Nor will the joy of the harp,
play of the song-beam,        nor the good hawk
swing through the hall,        nor the swift mare
stamp in the fortress-yard.        Wicked death
has sent forth        a multitude of mankind."
        Thus sad at heart        he complained of grief,
alone after all.        Sorrowful he wept
through day and night        until death's flood
touched his heart.        An old twilight-enemy
found the pleasure-hoard        standing open,
he who, burning,        seeks barrows,
naked evil-dragon,        who flies at night
encircled in fire.        Earth-dwellers
greatly dread him.        He must seek
a hoard in the ground        where, old in winters, he guards
heathen gold--        nor is he in any way better off for it.
Thus the enemy of the people        for three hundred winters
guarded in the ground        a certain hord-building,
the increasingly-crafty one,        until someone angered him,   2280
a man, in his heart.        To his liege-lord he bore
a plated cup,        a peace-compact
asked of his lord.        Thus was the hoard ransacked,
the hoard weakened of treasures,        and the request granted
to the destitute man.        The lord examined
the ancient work of men        for the first time.
        Then the worm awoke--        strife was renewed.
It stalked then along the stone;        the stark-hearted one
found its enemy's footprint.        He had stepped forth
with secret cunning        close by the head of the dragon.
So may an undoomed one        easily survive
woe and exile,        he who holds

the ruler's favor.     Readily along the ground[17]
the hoard-guardian searched,     wished to find the man,
the one who dealt foully     with him in his sleep.
Hot and fierce in mind     he often moved about the mound,
fully around the outside,     nor was anyone there
in that wilderness.     But he rejoiced in war,
in the work of battle.     Betimes he turned into the barrow
and sought the treasure-cup;     he soon perceived          2300
that a certain man     had found the gold,
the noble treasures.     The hoard-guardian
waited impatiently     until evening came;
then the barrow-keeper     was swollen with rage,
wished to requite     the enemy with fire
for the dear drinking-cup.     Then day was departed
according to the worm's wishes.     Nor within the walls
would he wait longer,     but went forth with flames,
with fire urged forward.     The source was terrible
for the people of the land,     as it was to be forthwith,
with respect to their treasure-giver,     disastrously ended.
          Then the visitant began     to spew flames,
to burn bright houses.     In the gleam of the fire
men stood in horror.     The loathed sky-flyer
wished to leave     nothing living there.
From the worm's fighting there was     widely seen
hard and hostile enmity     near and far,
how the battle-enemy     persecuted and humiliated
the people of the Geats.     He then shot back to the hoard,
secret noble-hall,     before daytime.                    2320
He had encircled with flame     the people of the land,
with fire and burning.     He trusted in the barrow,
in war and wall.     That expectation deceived him.
          Then to Beowulf     the horror was made known,

---

[17]Old English *Waldend* suggests God or a god, but may also imply simply "fate."

speedily, too truly,      because his own home,
best of dwellings,      melted in the fire-surgings,
gift-throne of the Geats.      To the good one that was
a grief in his heart,      greatest of mind-sorrows.
The wise one thought      that, with respect to the ruler,
eternal lord,      he had bitterly offended
against the old law.      His breast welled up inside
with dark thoughts,      as was not usual in him.
The fire-dragon      had crushed with flames
the fastness of the people,      the seashore without,
and the earth-work.      For that the war-king,
prince of the Weathers,      planned vengeance.
      The protector of warriors      commanded them to make,
lord of noblemen,      an adorned battle-shield
entirely of iron;      he knew certainly
that a wooden shield      could not help him,                     2340
linden-wood against fire.      The traverser of days,
ever-good nobleman,      must await the end
of life in the world,      and the worm also,
though he long held      the hoard-riches.
      The king of rings      then scorned
that he seek with a troop      the far-flyer,
with a vast army;      he did not dread the violence
for himself, nor the worm's warring,      for the creature did
deeds of strength and courage,      because before he often
had narrowly survived,      endured afflictions,
battle-clashes,      since he cleansed
Hrothgar's hall,      victory-blessed man,
and in battle crushed      Grendel's kin,
a loathed race.      Nor was that the least
of hand-encounters      where one slew Hygelac
after the king of the Geats      in the storm of battle,
friend-lord of the people,      in Frisian-lands,
Hrethel's son      died from the swords' drinking,
beaten by the blade.      Thence Beowulf came
by his own strength,      survived by swimming.                     2360

He had in his arms      the battle-garments
of thirty men      when he stepped toward the sea.
Not at all had the Hetware      reason for rejoicing,
for fighting on foot,      who against him bore
linden-shields before them.      Few came away afterwards
from that shield-soldier      to seek their home.
              The son of Ecgtheow      swam over the expanse of waters,
again to his people,      sad solitary one.
There Hygd offered him      treasure and kingdom,
rings and a princely throne.      She did not trust her son
that he knew how to hold      the ancestral throne
against foreign-folk      when Hygelac was dead.
None the sooner could      the destitute ones obtain
from the prince      in any way
that he become      the lord of Heardred
or that he would      accept the kingdom.
But he protected him among the people      with friendly advice, graciously with
honor,      until he became older
and ruled the Weather-Geats.      Exiles sought him
over the sea,      the sons of Ohtere.                            2380
They had rebelled against      the helm of the Scylfings,
the best      of sea-kings,
of those who dispensed treasure      in the Swedish kingdom,
a famous prince.      That became his end:
there for that care      he got a mortal-wound
from a sword's strokes,      the son of Hygelac;
and from them Ongentheow's son      afterwards departed
to seek his home      after Heardred lay dead,
let Beowulf hold      the princely throne,
to have power over the Geats.      That was a good king.
For that leader's-death he      remembered requital
in later days,      was a friend
to Eadgils in his poverty,      with an army supported
over the broad sea      the son of Ohtere
with warriors and weapons.      He wreaked vengeance after
with cold, dire exploits      deprived the king of life.

So he had survived          each one of his struggles,
of cruel clashes,          of courage-works,
the son of Ecgtheow,          until that one day
when he had to fight          against the worm.                          2400
The lord of the Geats then departed,          one among twelve,
enraged with anger,          to examine the dragon.
He had then heard          whence the feud arose,
baleful affliction of men.          Into his lap came
the famous treasure-cup          by the informant's hand.
In the troop he was          the thirteenth man,
who brought about          the onset of strife,
a slave sad in mind.          He had humbly thence
to lead the way to the plain.          Against his will he went
to that earth-hall which he          alone knew,
the barrow under ground          near the surging sea,
the tossing waves.          Inside it was full
of art and metal-works.          The ungentle guardian,
eager warrior,          held gold-treasures,
ancient under the earth.          Nor was that an easy bargain
to gain          for any man.
          The battle-hard king          then sat on the cliff,
bad good fortune          to hearth-companions,
gold-friend of the Geats.          His heart was sad,
restless and ready for death,          fate immeasurably near,          2420
the one whom men          must greet
to seek what is hidden in the soul,          to sever asunder
life from body.          Not at all long then was
the life of the prince          to be wound in the flesh.
Beowulf spoke,          Ecgtheow's son:
"In youth I survived          many battle-rushes,
times of fighting;          I remember all of that.
I was seven winters old          when the bold man of treasures,
friend-lord of the folk,          took me from my father.
King Hrethel          guarded and kept me,
gave me gift and feast,          remembered kinship.
Nor was I to him in life          more loathsome in anything,

man in the strongholds,      than any of his sons,
Herebeald and Haethcyn      or my Hygelac.
For the eldest,       unfittingly,
was the slaughter-bed strewn      by a kinsman's deeds,
after Haethcyn       struck down
his friend-lord,       with an arrow from his horn-bow,
missed the mark       and shot his kinsman dead,
the other brother       with a bloody point.                          2440
That was a recompense-less fight,      an ill-done evil,
heart-wearying in the breast;       however, the prince
must be deprived       of life unavenged.
Likewise it is sad       for an old man
to live to see       his son swing,
young on the gallows;       then he may recite a tale,
a sorrowful song,       when his son hangs,
a joy to the raven,       and he cannot help him,
old and knowing,       or do anything.
Always it is remembered,       each morning,
his son's journey elsewhere.       He is not intent
to live to see another [heir]       inside the dwellings,
a guardian of inheritance,       when the one has
experienced through deeds       death's insistence.
He looks sorrowfully       on his son's bower,
at the deserted wine-hall,       the windy resting-place,
reft of joy.       The riders sleep,
heroes in the hiding-place;       nor is there the harp-sound,
of pleasure in the courtyards,       such as there was before.
He departs then to bed,       sings a sorrowful lay,            2460
one after another;       it seems to him entirely too large,
fields and dwelling-place.       Likewise the helm of the Weathers:
sorrow was       in his heart for Herebeald,
a welling wave;       by no means could he
make amends with feud       on the life-slayer.
None the sooner could he       pursue the battle-warrior
with hostile deeds,       though he was not dear to him.
Then with that sorrow,       that which sorely befell him,

he gave up the joy of men,      chose god's light.
To his sons he left,      as does a fortunate man,
land and citadel,      when he departed from life.
          Then there was enmity and strife      of Swedes and Geats
over the wide water,      the common quarrel
of hard war-hatred      after Hrethel died,
and toward them Ongentheow's      sons were
brave, war-keen--      they did not wish to keep
friendship over the sea--      but near Hreosna Hill
often undertook      terrible, evil slaughter.
My friend-kinsman      avenged that
feud and wickedness,      as it was famed,                          2480
although the second one      paid with his life,[18]
a hard bargain.      To Haethcyn,
lord of the Geats,      that battle was deadly.
Then in the morning, I have heard,      the other kinsman[19]
took vengeance on the slayer      with the edges of the sword
when Ongentheow      seeks Eofor;
war-helm split,      the old Scylfing
fell, made pale by the sword.      The hand remembered
enough of the feud,      did not withhold the mortal-blow.
          I repaid with battle      those treasures
that he bestowed on me,      as it was given to me,
with the shining sword:      he granted me land,
a home, the joy of a homeland.      Nor had he any need
or good reason to seek,      buy at a price
a worse warrior      among the Gifthas
of the Spear-Danes      or in the Swedish-kingdom.
I would always go in front      of him in the foot-troop,
alone at the point,      and so I ever shall
do battle      while this sword endures,

---

[18]Haethcyn.

[19]Hygelac.

which often served me        before and after,                          2500
since before the veterans        I was the hand-slayer
of Daeghrafn,        champion of the Hugas.
Not at all could he        bring the treasure,
breast-ornament,        to the Frisian king,
but he fell in battle,        guardian of the standard,
nobleman with courage.        Nor was a sword his slayer,
but a battle-grip,        the heart's wellings,
broke his bone-house.        Now must the blade's edge,
hand and hard sword        fight over the hoard."
        Beowulf spoke,        uttered boastful-words
for the last time:        "I dared many
battles in youth,        yet I will,
old guardian of the people,        seek a feud,
do a glorious deed,        if the guilty enemy
will seek me outside        of the earth-hall."
Then he addressed        each of the men,
bold helm-bearers,        for the last time,
dear companions:        "I would not carry a sword,
a weapon against the worm        if I knew how
else I could        honorably grapple                          2520
with that terror,        as I did before against Grendel;[20]
but I expect the heat there        in the battle-fire
of the breath and the poison,        so I have on me
shield and byrnie.        Nor will I from the barrow-guardian
flee the space of one foot,        but between us two it must
be at the barrow        as fate bestows to us,
the ruler of each man.        I am hardy of heart,
so that against the battle-flyer        I refrain from boasts.
Wait on the barrow,        a band in byrnies,
men in armor,        which of the two can better,
after the slaughter-rush,        survive a wound,
of the two of us.        That is not your task,

---

[20]Here I have rendered *aglæcean* as "terror."

nor fitting for a man,      but mine alone,
unless against the powerful one      he deal out might,
do manly deeds.      With courage I must
gain the gold,      or battle will take me,
your lord,      terrible life-bale."
          The renowned warrior      arose then by the shield
hard under helm,      bore a war-corselet
under the stone-cliff,      trusted the strength                2540
of a single man:      such is not the coward's venture.
He saw then by the wall,      good in manly-customs,
he who survived      a great multitude of battles,
war-clashes      when foot-troops crash together,
a stream to issue thence      out of the stone-arch,
to burst forth from the barrow.      There was a burning rush
hot with battle-fires;      nor could he go near the hord
without burning,      at any time
endure the passageway      because of the dragon's fire.
The leader of the weather-Geats      then let a cry go out
from his breast,      when he was enraged:
the stout-hearted one roared.      The voice entered,
stormed battle-bright      under the gray stone.
          Hate was roused;      the hord-guardian heard
the man's voice.      Nor was there a greater time
to ask for peace.      First came
out from the stone      the breath of the beast,
hot battle-sweat;      the ground resounded.
The man under the barrow,      lord of the Geats,
swung his shield      toward the terror-guest.                2560
Then was the coiled-creature's      heart incited
to seek battle.      The good war-king
had already drawn his sword,      the old remnant
with edges not dull.      In each was,
intending destruction,      horror of the other.
          The strong-hearted one stood      behind the high shield,
leader of friends,      when the worm coiled
together immediately.      He waited in armor.

Then he moved, burning,      sank down gliding,
hastened toward destiny.      The shield guarded well
life and body      a lesser time
for the famous lord      than his hope sought;
there in that moment      for the first time
he must manage,      since fate did not appoint him
success in battle.      His hand swung up,
lord of the Geats;      the fearsome, shining one struck
with the remnant of battle-straits,      so that the edge failed,
bright on bone,      bit less strongly
than its king      had need of,
pressed under duress.      Then the barrow-keeper was,      2580
after the battle-stroke,      fierce in heart,
spewed deadly fire:      the war-flames
sprung widely.      The gold-friend of the Geats
did not boast of glorious-victory;      his war-blade had failed,
naked in battle,      as it never should,
ever-good iron one.      Nor was that an easy venture,
such that the famous one,      the son of Ecgtheow,
wished to abandon      the earth-plain,
should desire      to dwell in a home
elsewhere,      as each man must,
give up transitory days.      Nor was it long until
they met again,      the terrifying ones.
The hoard-guard heartened himself;      his breath welled
more quickly anew.      He suffered hardship,
encircled with fire,      he who before ruled the folk.
None at all from the troop      of close-comrades,
sons of noblemen,      stood nearby
in battle-excellence,      but they fled into the wood
to save their lives.      In one of them the heart
welled up with sorrows.      Kinship can never by any means      2600
be put aside      in him who thinks rightly.[21]

---

[21]Kinship is one of the themes of the poem.

Wiglaf he was called,        Weohstan's son,
beloved shield-warrior,       a prince of the Scylfings,
kinsman of Aelfhere.       He saw his liege-lord
under his war mask        suffer from the heat.
He remembered then the honors       that he gave him before,
wealthy homestead        of the Waegmundings,
each of the folk-rights,       just as his father had--
nor could he then hold back.        His hand seized shield,
yellow linden-wood;       he took the old sword
that was among men        "Eanmund's heirloom,"
son of Ohtere.        With that in battle
Weohstan was the slayer        with the sword's edge
of the friendless exile,        and carried to his kinsmen
the gleaming helm,        the ringed byrnie,
and the old giantish sword.        That Onela gave him,
the war-garments        of his relative,
ready battle-armor.        He spoke not at all of feud,
although he slew        the son of his brother.
He held the treasures        for many half-years,                    2620
sword and byrnie,        until his son was able
to do noble deeds        like his father before him.
Among the Geats he then gave him        war-garments,
a countless number of each,        when he departed from life,
old on the way forth.        Then was the first chance
for the young warrior,        that he must make
a battle-rush        with his noble lord;
his heart did not melt,        nor did his kinsman's relic
fail in war.        The worm found that out,
once they had        come together.
          Wiglaf spoke        many true words,
said them to his companions;        his heart was mournful.
"I remember that time        when we took mead,
when we promised        to our lord
in the beer-hall,        he who gave us these rings,
that in war-gear        we would repay him
if such need        befell him

of helmets and hard swords.     Thus he chose us for the army
for this venture     according to his own wishes,
deemed us worthy,     and gave me these treasures,          2640
because he accounted us     good spear-soldiers,
bold helm-bearers,     although the lord
intended alone     to perform
this valor-work,     guardian of the people,
because of men he has done     the most glorious acts,
impetuous deeds.     Now the day is come
when our liege-lord     has need of might,
of good battle-warriors;     let us go forward
to help the battle-leader,     while it may be,
against the grim fire-terror.     God knows
that to me it is much better     that with my gold-giver
the fire embrace     my body.
Nor does it seem proper to me     that we bear shields
home again     unless we can first
kill the blood-stained one,     defend the life
of the lord of the Geats.     I know certainly that
the merits of his former deeds     were not such that alone
of the veterans of the Geats     he should suffer,
fall in battle.     Among us must sword and helmet,
byrnie and battle-gear,     in both be shared."          2660
        He went then through the battle-vapor,     bore battle-helm,
in support of the lord,     and spoke a few words:
"Beloved Beowulf,     fulfill all well,
as in the span of youth     you readily have said
that you would never let,     while you were living,
your glory diminish.     Now with famous deeds,
resolute prince,     with all your strength
you must defend your life.     I will help you."
        After those words     the worm came in anger,
monstrous malice-guest,     a second time
with fire-surgings shining     to seek its enemies,
the loathed men.     The fire flowed in waves,
burnt up the shield to the rim;     the byrnie could not

provide help      for the young spear-warrior,
but the young kinsman      went with courage
under his kinsman's shield      when his own was
consumed in flames.      Then yet the war-king
remembered glory,      with might-strength struck
with battle-blade      so that it stood in the head,
compelled by ferocity:      Naegling burst,                    2680
failed in battle,      Beowulf's sword,
old and gray.      To him it was not given
that edges      of iron could
help in battle:      the hand was too strong,
that which with a stroke,      I have heard,
overtaxed each sword      when he to battle bore
weapons hard with wounds,      nor was he any the better for them.
      Then the enemy of the people was      for a third time
mindful of the feud,      fearsome fire-dragon.
He rushed the renowned one      when the chance was granted him,
hot and battle-grim,      completely clasped the neck,
the bones of the fierce one.      He was bloodied
with soul's-blood:      the fluid welled in waves.
      Then in his need I have heard      of the king
that the man at his side      showed courage,
skill and boldness,      as was natural to him.
Nor did he heed that head,      but the hand
of the brave man was burned      when he helped his kinsman
because he struck the evil-guest      somewhat farther down,
man in armor,      so that the sword dived in,                    2700
shining and gold-coated,      such that the fire began
to abate afterwards.      Then the king himself yet
ruled his senses,      drew his slaughter-knife,
bitter and battle-sharp,      that he bore in his byrnie.
The protector of Weathers cut      the worm through the middle.
The enemy fell--      courage avenged life--
and they both      had killed him,
the noble kinsmen.      So should a man be,
a thane at need.      For the king that was

the last victory-time     of his own deeds,
of work in the world.     Then the wound began,
which the earth-dragon     had previously made in him,
to burn and swell.     He soon realized
that in his breast     a grievous evil welled up,
poison on the inside.     Then the prince went,
wise-hearted one,     so that by the wall
he sat on a seat.     He saw in the giant-work
how the stone-arch     held the inside,
eternal earth-hall,     with pillars.
Then with his hands     the immeasurably good thane          2720
laved with water     the savagely bleeding
famous king,     his friend-lord
wearied with battle,     and unfastened his helmet.

      Beowulf spoke--     despite the injury spoke,
mortal-misery.     He knew truly
that he had     completed his time,
joys in the world;     then was his number of days
entirely passed,     death immeasurably near.
"Now I to my son     would wish to give
war-garments,     had there been given such,
had any heir     come after[22]
related in body.     I ruled the people
for fifty winters,     nor was there a king of the people
of surrounding nations,     any of them,
who dared meet me     with battle-friends,
to threaten me with fear.     In the land I awaited
my fated-time,     held my own well,
nor sought cunning enmities,     nor wrongfully swore
many oaths.     Weak with mortal wounds,
in all of this I can     have joy,          2740
so the ruler of men     need not reproach me
for the evil-murder of kinsmen     when my life

---

[22]The word means more specifically "inheritance-guardian" than "heir."

departs from the body.       Now go quickly
to examine the hoard       under the gray stone,
beloved Wiglaf,       now the worm lies dead,
sleeps sorely wounded,       bereft of treasure.
Be now in haste       so that I may see
the ancient-wealth,       fully behold
the sparkling, artful gems,       so that I can more gently,
after the treasure-wealth,       give up my
life and country,       which I held long."
        Then, I have heard, quickly       after the word-speech
of the wounded lord,       the son of Weohstan,
to obey the battle-sick one       bore his ring-net,
broad battle-byrnie       under the barrow's roof.
The victory-triumphing one,       brave young-thane,
saw when he went by the seat       many treasure-jewels,
gold shining       near on the ground,
wonders on the wall,       and in the worm's den,
that of the old twilight-flyer,       cups standing,              2760
vessels of men of old       lacking a polisher,
bereft of ornaments.       There was many a helmet,
old and rusty,       many an arm-ring
tied artfully.       Treasure can
easily overcome       each of the race of men,
gold in the ground,       heed this he who will.[23]
Also he saw resting       an entirely golden standard
high over the hord,       greatest of hand-made wonders,
interlocked with hand-skill;       lights stood out from it,
so that he could see       the ground-floor,
search the artworks.       Nor was there any sign
of the worm there,       for the sword took him.
        Then I have heard in the mound       one man
plundered the hoard,       old work of giants,
loaded into his arms       goblets and dishes

---

[23]Another theme of the poem:  the dangers of greed.

of his own choice.          He also took the standard,
brightest of beacons.          The blade before had hurt,
edge of iron,          the ancient-lord
who was protector          of the treasures
for a long while,          who carried on fire-terror               2780
with heat before the hoard,          fiercely welling up
in the middle of the night--          until he died for murder.
          The messenger was in haste,          eager for return,
urged forward with booty.          Anxiety burst from him
about whether he would find alive          the bold-spirited one
in that place,          king of the Weathers,
deprived of power,          where he had left him before.
Then with the treasures          he found bloody
his lord,          the famous king,
at the end of his life.          He again began
to splash him with water,          until the point of a word
broke through the breast-hoard.          Then the man spoke,
old among youths,          beheld the gold:
"For those treasures I          thank the lord of all,
the king of glory,          say in words
to the eternal lord,          for what I stare upon,
that I was able          to win such
for my people          before my death-day.
Now that for the hord of treasures          I have sold
the old portion of life,          attend henceforth               2800
to the need of the people.          I can no longer be here.
Command the battle-famed ones          to make a barrow,
bright after the fire,          at the sea's headland.
That shall for remembrances          among my people
rise high          on the Whale's Cliff,
so that seafarers          afterwards will call it
Beowulf's Barrow          when ships
drive far away          over the darkness of the sea."
          He took from his neck          the golden ring,
bold-hearted king,          gave it to the thane,
to the young spear-warrior,          and the gold-adorned helmet,

ring and byrnie,      commanded him to enjoy them well:
"You are the last      of our race,
of the Waegmundings;      fate has lured away
all my kinsmen      according to the measurer's decree,
men in valor.      I must [go] after them."
          That was the last word      from the old one's
heart-thoughts,      before he accepted the fire,
hot battle-surgings;      from his breast the soul
departed to seek      the judgment of the just.                    2820
          When it had gone      so grievously
for the not-old man,      that on earth he saw
the dearest one's      life at an end,
he fared miserably.      The killer also lay [dead],
dreadful earth-dragon,      bereft of life,
driven to destruction.      Over treasure hords
the coiled worm      could not rule long,
but the iron one,      the edge took him,
the hard battle-scarred      remnant of hammers,
so that the wide-flyer's corpse,      still from wounds,
[lay] on the ground      near the hoard-hall.
Never afterwards in the sky      moving quickly might he turn
in the middle of the night,      proud of treasure-possessions
to show his countenance,      but he had fallen to earth
before the hand-work      of that battle-leader.
Truly in that land      few men prospered,
possessers of power,      I have heard,
though one were bold      in each of his deeds,
such that he rushed upon the breath      of the venomous foe
or with hands plundered      the ring-hall                    2840
if he found      the guardian waking,
inhabiting the barrow.      To Beowulf an allotment
of noble-treasures      was in death repaid.
Each had      reached the end

of a transitory life.        Nor was it long then[24]
till the battle-cowards        quit the woods,
weak troth-breakers,        ten together,
When they dared not before        fight with javelins
in their liege-lord's        great need,
but feeling ashamed they        carried shields,
battle-garments        to where the old one lay,
and looked at Wiglaf.        He sat wearied,
foot-warrior,        by the shoulder of his lord,
tried to revive him with water,        by no means succeeded;
nor could he on earth,        though he wished well,
preserve the life        of the chief-spearman,
nor change anything        of the ruler's [decree].
The judgment of god        would govern the deeds
of every man,        as it yet does now.
        Then from the young one        a grim answer                2860
was quickly obtained        for him who had lost courage before.
Wiglaf spoke,        Weohstan's son;
the man, sad at heart,        looked at the unloved:
"Lo, he may say,        who will tell the truth,
that the liege-lord        who gave you those treasures,
cavalry-gear,        in which you stand there,
that when he often gave        on the ale-bench
helmet and byrnie        to the hall-sitters,
a king to his thanes,        such as most splendid
he could find        anywhere, far or near,
he completely,        grievously threw away
those battle-garments        when his war arose.
Not at all did the king of the people        need to boast
about war-companions;        however, god granted him,
ruler of victories,        that he avenge himself
alone with the sword        when he had need of courage.
Little life-protection        could I

---

[24]Another theme: life is transitory.

give him in battle,      but nevertheless began
beyond my power      to help my kinsman.
Steadily was it the weaker      when I struck with my sword      2880
the mortal-foe,      the fire boiling
less strongly from its head.      Too few defenders
thronged around the king      when his time of need had come.
Now treasure-getting      and sword-giving,
all the homeland-joys      of your race,
love, must cease.      Each one of the men
of the group of kinsmen      must go deprived
of land-rights,      when noblemen
far away will hear of      your flight,
a glory-less deed.      Death is better
for each man      than a life of reproach."
He then ordered that battle-work      announced at the encampment
beyond the cliff-edge      where that troop of men
a long-morninged day      sat sad at heart,
shield in hand,      in expectation of both
day's end      and the return
of the beloved man.      Not at all was he silent
of news, the messenger      who rode to the headland,
but he truly      spoke to all.
           "Now is the wish-giver,      leader of the Weathers,      2900
lord of the Geats,      fast in his death-bed,
dwells in slaughter-rest      because of the worm's deeds.
Beside him lies      the life-enemy,
sick with knife-gashes.      With the sword he could not
by any means      cause a wound
in that monster.      Wiglaf sits,
son of Weohstan,      over Beowulf,
one man by the other      unliving,
holds with heart-weariness      head-watch over
beloved man and enemy.      Now for the nation is expectation
of war-time      when widely
among Franks and Frisians      the fall of the king
is uncovered.      That strife was created,

hard against the Hugas,       after Hygelac came
to travel with a sea-army       into the land of the Frisians,
where the Hetware       attacked him in battle,
approached with courage       and superior strength,
so that the byrnied warrior       must bow:
he fell among the foot-troop.       He did not give treasures,
leader to his veterans.       Never afterwards                    2920
did the Merovingians       grant us kindness.
Nor do I by any means expect       peace or troth
from the Swedish people,       but it was widely known
that Ongentheow       deprived Haethcyn of life,
Hrethel's son,       near Ravenswood,
when from arrogance       they, war-Scylfings,
first sought out       the people of the Geats.
Soon the old one,       father of Ohtere
ancient and terrible,       gave him a counterstrike,
destroyed the sea-king,       rescued his wife,
old noblewoman       bereft of gold,
Onela's mother       and Ohtere's,
and then pursued       [his] mortal-foes
until they escaped       with difficulty
into Ravenswood,       lordless.
He besieged then with a vast army       what swords had left
weary with wounds,       often threatened woes
to the wretched band       all night long,
said in the morning       with the edges of the sword
he would make [blood] flow,       some on the gallows-tree       2940
[leave] as sport for birds.       Comfort came after
for the sad-hearted ones       just at daybreak
when they together       heard Hygelac's
horn and trumpet,       when the good one came
with the veterans of the nation       going behind him.
The bloody track       of Swedes and Geats,
slaughter-rush of men,       was widely visible,
how the folk with him       awoke a feud.
The good one himself then left,       the noble Ongentheow,

with his companions,     old and very mournful,
to seek a stronghold,     went further up.
He had heard      of Hygelac in battle,
of the proud one's war-skill,     did not trust in resistance,
that he could      oppose the seamen,
against the seafaring-warriors     defend hord,
child, and bride.     He fled thence afterwards,
old one, under the earth-wall.     Then pursuit was offered
upon the people of the Swedes.     Hygelac's banner
traversed forward      over the peace-plain
until the Hrethlings     thronged upon the entrenchment.     2960
There was Ongentheow,     gray-haired one,
with the edges of the sword     compelled to stop,
so that the king of the people     must submit
to Eofor's own judgment.     Angrily, Wulf,
Wonred's son,     struck him with a weapon,
so that from that stroke     blood sprung forth in streams
from under his hair.     Nor was he frightened so,
the old Scylfing,     but repaid quickly
that murderous-blow     with a worse exchange
when the king of the people     turned thither.
Nor could the bold one,     son of Wonred,
give a counterblow     to the old man,
for on his head     it had cut through the helmet
so that, blood-stained,     he must bow down,
fell on the ground--     he was not doomed yet,
but he recovered himself,     though that wound touched him.
The hardy [Eofer],     Hygelac's thane,
let [his] broad sword,     when his brother lay still,
old giantish sword,     break the giant-helm
over the shield-wall.     Then the king buckled,     2980
guardian of the people,     was struck mortally.
     Then many bound     his kinsman's wounds,
who speedily raised him up     when there was space for them
because they could control     the battle-place.
Meanwhile, one warrior     plundered another,

took from Ongentheow      the iron byrnie,
a hard, hilted sword,      and his helmet together.
One carried      the gray armor to Hygelac.
He grasped the treasures      and fairly promised
to reward him before the people,      and he performed it so:
the lord of the Geats      repaid the battle-rush,
Hrethel's son,      when he had come home,
Eofor and Wulf      with immense treasure,
gave each of them      a hundred thousand
of land and locked-rings--      nor needed a man in middle-earth
reproach  him  for  that  reward,      since  he  won  those  glories  by
                    fighting.
Then he gave to Eofor      his only daughter,
an honor to his home,      in pledge of friendship.
            That is the feud      and the enmity,
deadly-evil of men,      because of which I expect            3000
that the people of the Swedes      will seek us out
after they find      our lord
is lifeless,      the one who before held
hoard and kingdom      against enemies,
[who] after the fall of heroes,      valiant Scyldings,
accomplished aid for the folk      or further still
did noble deeds.      Now haste is best,
that there we look upon      the king of the people
and then bring [him],      who gave us rings,
on the way to the pyre.      Nor must a part only
melt with the brave one there,      but the hoard of treasures,
countless gold      grimly purchased,
and now at the last      with his own life
are the rings bought.      The burning shall consume,
the fire enfold them,      nor will a man wear
the treasures as memorials,      nor a beautiful maid
have on her throat      a noble circlet,
but the one sad-in-heart,      bereft of gold,
must often, by no means once,      travel foreign lands,
now that the battle-leader      has laid down laughter,      3020

sport and song-joy.       Therefore must many a spear,
morning-cold,       be enclosed in palms,
hefted in hands,       not at all the sound of the harp
rouse warriors,       but the black raven,
eager over the dead,       speak many [things],
say to the eagle       how he hastened at eating
when he and the wolf       plundered corpses."
          Thus the brave man       was telling
loathed tales;       he did not falsify
destinies or words.       The troop all arose,
went unhappily       under Eagle's Cliff
with gushing tears       to behold the wonder.
They found then on the sand       the soul-less one,
the death-bed of the guardian,       the one who gave them rings
in former times.       Then was the last day
of the good one reached,       in which the war-king,
lord of the Weathers,       died a wondrous death.
They had seen before       the strange creature,
the worm on the plain       right opposite there,
lying by his enemy.       The fire-dragon,                           3040
fierce, terror-shining one,       had been swallowed in flames.
He was fifty       foot-paces
long in his resting-place.       In the joyous air he ruled
at one time by night,       departed after downward
to seek his den.       He was then fast in death,
had enjoyed earth-caves       for the last time.
Beside him stood       goblets and cups;
dishes lay [there]       and precious swords,
rusty, eaten through,       as in the bosom of the earth
they dwelt there       a thousand winters.
Then was that inheritance,       gold of men of old,
with exceeding-skill       encompassed with incantation,
so that no man       could reach
that ring-hall       unless god himself,
truth-king of victories,       gave it to whom he wished--
his is the protection of people--       to open the hoard,

even to whichever man      to him seemed fitting.
    ● Then it was visible      that the venture did not prosper
for the one who wrongfully      had hidden treasures
inside under the wall.      The keeper earlier slew            3060
a certain one of the few;      then that feud was
grievously avenged.      It is a wonder when
a brave man      reaches the end
of allotted life;      then he can no longer
dwell in the mead-hall,      one among his kinsmen.
So it was with Beowulf      when he sought hostilities
with the barrow's guardian;      he himself did not know
through what [means] his severing from the world      must occur.
So until judgment day,      famous lords
had solemnly pronounced      when [they] placed it there,
that the man would be,      he who plundered it,
guilty with sins,      imprisoned in idol-groves,
fast in hell-bonds      tormented grievously.
Not at all had he more readily      examined before
the owner's legacy,      gold-enchanted place.[25]
      Wiglaf spoke,      Weohstan's son:
"Often shall many a man      by the will of one
endure exile,      as it has come to pass for us.
Nor could we persuade      the beloved king,
keeper of the kingdom,      by any counsel            3080
that he not attack      the gold-guardian,
let him lie      where he long was,
to remain in his home      till the end of the world.
He held to noble-destiny.      The hoard is shown,
terribly got.      What was destined was too strong,
that which thither      impelled the king.
I was there inside      and looked over all that,
the treasures of the hall,      when it was granted to me,
not at all in a friendly fashion,      access granted

---

[25]Old English *gold-hwæte*, "gold-abounding" or perhaps "gold-accursed."

in under the earth-wall.      In haste I seized
with my hands a large,      mighty burden
of hoard-treasures,      hither outside bore it
to my king.      He was then still alive,
sound in mind and conscious.      He spoke a multitude in all,
old and grieving,      commanded me to greet you,
bade that you build      for the deeds of your friend
on the place of the pyre      the high barrow,
great and famous,      since of men he was
the worthiest warrior      widely through the earth,
while he could enjoy      the wealth of the citadel.            3100
From without now let us hasten      on a second journey
to see and seek      heaps of precious stones,
a wonder under the wall.      I will lead you
so that sufficiently near      you [may] behold
the rings and broad gold.      So that the pyre be ready,
[let it be] quickly prepared      when we come out,
and then carry      our lord,
beloved man,      where he must
long dwell      in the ruler's protection."
          He then commanded ordered,      son of Weohstan,
battle-dear hero,      to many of the warriors,
the home-owners,      that they bring from far
pyre-wood      for the chief of the people,
toward the good one:      "Now must the fire consume,
the flame grow dark,      the prince of warriors,
the one who often endured      showers of iron
when a storm of arrows      impelled by bow-strings
rushed over the shield-wall,      the shaft held to its duty,
eager in feathers,      following the arrow."
          Indeed the wise one,      son of Weohstan,                  3120
called forth from the band      of the king's thanes
seven together,      the best;
he went one of eight      under the evil-roof,
battle-warrior.      One in his hands bore
a fire-torch,      he who went in front.

Nor was it then by lot      who [should] plunder that hoard,
since lacking a guardian,      any portion
the men saw      remaining in the hall
lay temporarily.      Little any of them mourned
that they hastily      carried out
the precious treasures.      The dragon also they shoved,
the worm, over the cliff,      let the waves take him,
the sea embrace      the keeper of treasures.
Then was the twisted gold      loaded on a wagon,
a countless number of everything,      and the prince borne,
gray battle-warrior,      to Whale's Cliff.
      For him the people of the Geats      made ready
on the ground a funeral pyre      not ignoble,
hung with helmets      and battle-shields,
with bright byrnies,      according to the boon he asked.      3140
They laid in the midst      the famous lord,
lamenting the hero,      the beloved lord.
They began then on the cliff      to awaken for the warrior
the greatest of pyres.      Wood-smoke ascended,
black over the fire,      the flame roaring,
wound round with weeping--      The wind-tumult subsided--
until it had broken      the bone-house,
hot to the heart.      With miserable spirits,
with heart-sorrow they mourned      their liege-lord's death;
likewise with a lament      a Geatish woman
. . . [sang]      with hair bound up[26]
a [song] of sorrow-care.      She told often
that she herself sorely      dreaded invasions,
a multitude of slaughters,      the horrors of the host,
humiliation and captivity.      Heaven swallowed the smoke.
      The people of the Weathers      then built
a mound on the cliff      that was high and broad,

---

[26]Some additional trouble spots appear in the manuscript from here to the end.

widely visible      to seafarers,
and [they] built      in ten days
the battle-bold one's monument.      With the flame's remnants 3160
they surrounded the wall,      as the worthiest,
very wise men      could devise it.
In the mound they placed      rings and jewels,
all such ornaments      as from the hoard previously
cruel-minded men      had taken away.
They left the treasure of men      for the earth to hold,
gold in the sand,      where it now yet dwells,
just as useless to men      as it was before.
Then they rode round the mound      of the battle-dear one,
sons of noblemen,      twelve in all,
wished to talk with care,      to tell of the king,
recite a lay,      to speak about the man,
praised his nobility      and deeds of valor,
by the veterans lauded.      Thus it is fitting
that one praise in words      his friend-lord,
love in spirit,      when he must
be led forth      from the body.
          The people of the Geats      thus grieved
their lord,      hearth-companions:
they said that he was,      of the kings of the world,      3180
to men the mildest      and most gentle,
to his people the kindest,      and most eager for fame.

# Selected Bibliography

## EDITIONS

Chickering, Howell D., Jr., ed. *Beowulf: A Dual Language Edition.*
Anchor Books. Garden City, NY: Anchor/Doubleday, 1977.
(Includes a translation.)

Dobbie, Elliott van Kirk., ed. *Beowulf and Judith.* The Anglo-
Saxon Poetic Records, Vol 4. New York: Columbia UP, 1953.

Klaeber, Friedrich, ed. *Beowulf and the Fight at Finnsburg.* 3rd
ed. Boston: Heath, 1950.

Wrenn, C. L., ed. *Beowulf with the Finnesburg Fragment.* Revised
W. F. Bolton. London: Harrap, 1973.

Zupitza, Julius, ed. *Beowulf: British Museum MS. Cotton Vitellius
A xv (Facsimile).* 2nd. ed. Early English Text Society 245.
London: Oxford UP, 1959.

## SUGGESTED TRANSLATIONS

Alexander, Michael, trans. *Beowulf.* Harmondsworth: Penguin,
1973.

Bradley, S. A. J., trans. *Beowulf.* In *Anglo-Saxon Poetry: An
Anthology of Old English Poems in Prose Translation with
Introduction and Headnotes by S. A. J. Bradley.* Everyman's
Library. London and Melbourne: Dent, 1982. 408-94.

Crossley-Holland, Kevin, trans. *Beowulf.* Intro. Bruce Mitchell.
New York: Farrar, Strauss & Giroux, 1968.

Donaldson, E. Talbot. *Beowulf: A New Prose Translation.* New
York: Norton, 1966.

Greenfield, Stanley B, trans. *A Readable Beowulf.* Intro. Alain Renoir. Carbondale and Edwardsville: Southern Illinois UP, 1982.

Hudson, Marc, trans. *Beowulf: A Translation and Commentary.* Lewisburg, PA: Bucknell UP; London and Toronto: Associated UP, 1990.

Huppé, Bernard F. *Beowulf: A New Translation.* Pegasus Paperbooks Series, Vol. 1. Binghamton: Medieval and Renaissance Texts and Studies, 1987.

Kennedy, Charles, trans. *Beowulf.* New York: Oxford UP, 1940.

Lehmann, Ruth P. M., trans. *Beowulf: An Imitative Translation.* Austin: U of Texas P, 1988.

Morgan, Edwin, trans. *Beowulf: A Verse Translation into Modern English.* Berkeley, Los Angeles, London: U of California P, 1952. (Includes a review of earlier translations.)

Osborne, Marijane, trans. *Beowulf: A Verse Translation with Treasures of the Ancient North.* Berkeley: U of California P, 1983.

Rebsamen, Frederick. *Beowulf: A Verse Translation.* New York: Harper Collins, 1991.

Swearer, Randolph, Raymond Oliverand Marijane Osborne. *Beowulf: A Likeness.* New Haven and London: Yale UP, 1990.

Tinker, Chauncey B. *The Translations of Beowulf: A Critical Bibliography.* Yale Studies in English 16. New York: Gordian, 1967. (Not a translation, but reviews pre-1902 translations.)

BIBLIOGRAPHIES

*Anglo-Saxon England.* Ed. Peter Clomoes. Cambridge: Cambridge UP. (Annual)

Chambers, R. W. *Beowulf: An Introduction.* 3rd ed. with supplement by C. L. Wrenn. London: Cambridge UP, 1959.

Fry, Donald K. *Beowulf and the Fight at Finnsburh: A Bibliography.* Charlottesville: U of Virginia P, 1969.

*MLA International Bibliography.* New York:   Modern Language
     Association of America.  Annual.  (See Volume I for the year's
     works on *Beowulf* and related topics.)
*Old English Newsletter.*  Journal of the Center for Medieval and
     Renaissance Studies at the State University of New York at
     Binghamton.  (Publishes annual issue reviewing the year's
     studies in Old English, with a section on *Beowulf.*)
Robinson, Fred C.  *Old English Literature:  A Select Bibliography.*
     Toronto:  U of Toronto P, 1970.
Short, Douglas.  *Beowulf Scholarship:  An Annotated Bibliography.*
     Garland Reference Library of the Humanities 193.  New York:
     Garland, 1980.


STUDIES AND BACKGROUND


Abels, Richard P.  *Lordship and Military Obligation in Anglo-Saxon
     England.*  Berkeley and London:  U of California P, 1988.
Bartlett, Adeline Courtney.  *The Larger Rhetorical Patterns in
     Anglo-Saxon Poetry.*  New York:  Columbia UP, 1935.
Bateson, F. W.  *English Poetry and the English Language.*  Oxford:
     Clarendon, 1973.
Benson, Larry D.  "The Pagan Coloring of *Beowulf.*"  *Old English
     Poetry:  Fifteen Essays.*  Ed. Robert P. Creed.  Providence,
     RI:  Brown UP, 1967.  193-213.
Blair, Peter Hunter.  *An Introduction to Anglo-Saxon England.*  2nd
     ed.  Cambridge:  Cambridge UP, 1977.
Bonjour, Adrien.  *The Digressions in Beowulf.*  Oxford:  Blackwell,
     1950.
Bradley, S. A. J.  *Anglo-Saxon Poetry.*  Everyman's Library.  London
     and Melbourne:  Dent, 1982.
Brodeur, Arthur G.  *The Art of Beowulf.*  Berkeley:  U of California
     P, 1959.
Bronsted, Johannes.   *The Vikings.*   Trans. Kalle Skov.   Harmondsworth:
     Penguin, 1973.

Bruce-Mitford, R. L. S. *The Sutton Hoo Ship Burial: Reflections after Thirty Years*. Centre for Medieval Studies. York, England: W. Sessions, 1979.

Cable, Thomas. *The Meter and Melody of Beowulf*. London: U of Illinois P, 1974.

Carver, M. O. H., ed. *The Age of Sutton Hoo: The Seventh Century in North-Western Europe*. Woodbridge, Suffolk; Rochester, NY: Boydell, 1992.

Chance, Jane. *Woman as Hero in Old English Literature*. Syracuse: Syracuse UP, 1986.

Chase, Colin, ed. *The Dating of Beowulf*. Toronto Old English Series 6. Toronto: U of Toronto P, 1981. (Anthology)

Clark, George. Beowulf. Boston: Twayne, 1990.

Creed, Robert P, ed. *Old English Poetry: Fifteen Essays*. Providence: Brown UP, 1967.

Damico, Helen. *Beowulf's Wealhtheow and the Valkyrie Tradition*. Madison: U of Wisconsin P, 1984.

Dronke, Ursula. "*Beowulf* and Ragnarok." *Saga-Book of the Viking Society* 17 (1969): 302-25.

Fajardo-Acosta, Fidel. *The Condemnation of Heroism in the Tragedy of Beowulf: A Study in the Characterization of Epic*. Studies in Epic and Romance Literature 2. Lewiston, NY: Edwin Mellen, 1989.

Frank, Roberta. " The *Beowulf* Poet's Sense of History." *The Wisdom of Poetry: Essays in Early English Literature in Honor of Morton W. Bloomfield*. Ed. Larry D. Benson and Siegfried Wenzel. Kalamazoo: Medieval Institute Publications, 1982. 53-65, 271-77.

Frantzen, Allen J. ed. *Speaking Two Languages: Traditional Disciplines and Contemporary Theory in Medieval Studies*. Albany: SUNY P, 1991. (Useful for students with some background or interest in contemporary literary theory.)

Garmonsway, G. N., Jacqueline Simpson and Hilda Ellis Davidson. *Beowulf and Its Analogues*. London: Dent, 1968.

Gatch, Milton McC. *Loyalties and Traditions: Man and His World in Old English Literature.* Pegasus Backgrounds in English Literature. New York: Bobbs-Merrill, 1971.

Godden, Malcolm, and Michael Lapidge, eds. *Cambridge Companion to Old English Literature.* Cambridge: Cambridge UP, 1991. (Excellent material on *Beowulf* and other OE topics.)

Goldsmith, Margaret. *The Mode and Meaning of Beowulf.* London: Aethlone, 1970.

Green, Martin. "Man, Time, and Apocalypse in *The Wanderer, The Seafarer,* and *Beowulf.*" *Journal of English and Germanic Philology* 74 (1975): 502-18.

Greenfield, Stanley B., and Daniel G. Calder. *A New History of Old English Literature.* With a survey of the Anglo-Latin background by Michael Lapidge. New York and London: New York UP, 1986.

Haarder, Andreas. *Beowulf: The Appeal of a Poem.* Copenhagen: Akademisk Forlag, 1975.

Hoover, David L. *A New Theory of Old English Meter.* American University Studies 4, English Language and Literature 14. New York, Bern, Frankfurt am Main, Paris: Peter Lang, 1985.

Hume, Kathryn. "The Theme and Structure of *Beowulf.*" *Studies in Philology* 72 (1975): 1-27.

Huppé, Bernard F. *The Hero in the Earthly City: A Reading of Beowulf.* Medieval and Renaissance Texts and Studies 33. Binghamton: Center for Medieval and Renaissance Studies, 1984.

Irving, Edward B. Jr. *A Reading of Beowulf.* New Haven: Yale UP, 1968.

---. *Rereading Beowulf.* University of Pennsylvania Press Middle Ages Series. Philadelphia: U of Pennsylvania P, 1986.

Kiernan, Kevin S. *Beowulf and the Beowulf Manuscript.* New Brunswick: Rutgers UP, 1981.

Lawrence, William W. *Beowulf and the Epic Tradition.* 1928. New York: Hafner, 1961.

Lee, Alvin. *The Guest-Hall of Eden: Four Essays on the Design of Old English Poetry.* New Haven: Yale UP, 1972.

Lyerle, John. "The Interlace Structure of *Beowulf*." *University of Toronto Quarterly* 37 (1967): 1-17.

Magoun, Francis P., Jr. "The Oral-Formulaic Character of Anglo-Saxon Narrative Poetry." *Speculum* 28 (1953): 446-67.

Nicholson, Lewis A., ed. *An Anthology of Beowulf Criticism*. Notre Dame: Notre Dame UP, 1963. (Perhaps the best anthology of essays on *Beowulf*. Includes essays by Baum, Blackburn, Bloomfield, Cabaniss, Chadwick, Goldsmith, Hamilton, Kaske, Malone, Magoun, McNamee, Robertson, Rogers, Schücking, and Tolkien, Wrenn, and Wright.)

Niles, John D. *Beowulf: the Poem and Its Tradition*. Cambridge, MA, and London: Harvard UP, 1983.

---. "Rewriting *Beowulf*: The Task of Translation." *College English* 55.8 (1993): 858-77.

Parker, Mary A. *Beowulf and Christianity*. American University Studies, Series 4, English Language and Literature 51. New York, Bern, Frankfurt am Main, Paris: Peter Lang, 1987.

Pope, John C. *The Rhythm of Beowulf*. Revised ed. New Haven: Yale UP, 1968.

Puhvel, Martin. *Beowulf and the Celtic Tradition*. Waterloo, Ontario: Wilfrid Laurier UP, 1979.

Risden, Edward L. *Beasts of Time: Apocalyptic Beowulf*. Studies in the Humanities 8. New York, Bern, Frankfurt am Main, Paris: Peter Lang, 1994.

Robinson, Fred C. *Beowulf and the Appositive Style*. Knoxville: U of Tennessee P, 1985.

Shippey, T. A. *Beowulf*. London: Edward Arnold, 1978.

Sisam, Kenneth. *The Structure of Beowulf*. Oxford: Clarendon, 1965.

Tillyard, E. M. W. *The English Epic and Its Background*. 1954. New York: Oxford UP, 1966.

Tolkien, J. R. R. "*Beowulf*: The Monsters and the Critics." *Proceedings of the British Academy* 22 (1936): 245-95. Reprinted in Nicholson 51-103.

Watts, Ann C. *The Lyre and the Harp: A Comparative Reconsideration of Oral Tradition in Homer and Old English Epic Poetry*. Yale Studies in English 168. New Haven: Yale UP, 1969.

Whitelock, Dorothy. *The Audience of Beowulf*. Oxford: Clarendon, 1951.

Williams, David. *Cain and Beowulf: A Study in Secular Allegory*. Toronto, Buffalo, and London: U of Toronto P, 1982.

Wilson, David M. *Anglo-Saxon Art from the Seventh Century to the Norman Conquest*. Woodstock, NY: Overlook P, 1984.

Wood, Michael. *In Search of the Dark Ages*. New York: Facts on File, 1987.

Wrenn, C. L. *A Study of Old English Literature*. New York: Norton, 1967.